In the Footsteps
of Davy Crockett

Other *In the Footsteps*™ *Series* Titles

In the Footsteps of Daniel Boone by Randell Jones
In the Footsteps of Robert E. Lee by Clint Johnson
In the Footsteps of Stonewall Jackson by Clint Johnson
In the Footsteps of J. E. B. Stuart by Clint Johnson

In the Footsteps
of Davy Crockett

by Randell Jones

John F. Blair, Publisher  Winston-Salem, North Carolina

*The paper in this book meets the guidelines
for permanence and durability of the Committee on
Production Guidelines for Book Longevity
of the Council on Library Resources.*

COVER IMAGE
David Crockett, oil on canvas painted by William Henry Huddle (1889)
Courtesy of The State Preservation Board, Austin, Texas

Library of Congress Cataloging-in-Publication Data
Jones, K. Randell.
p.   cm. — (In the footsteps series)
Includes bibliographical references and index.
ISBN-13: 978-0-89587-324-8 (alk. paper)
ISBN-10: 0-89587-324-9
1. Crockett, Davy, 1786-1836—Homes and haunts—Southern States. 2.
Crockett, Davy, 1786-1836—East (U.S.) 3. Historic sites—Southern
States—Guidebooks. 4. Historic sites—East (U.S.)—Guidebooks. 5.
Southern States—Guidebooks. 6. East (U.S.)—Guidebooks. 7. Southern
States—History, Local. 8. East (U.S.)—History, Local. I. Title. II. Series
F436.C95J66   2006
976.8'04092—dc22   2006000088

Design by Debra Long Hampton

For Dad,
another American hero—US Navy, WWII, Purple Heart

For Mother,
who sewed me Davy Crockett pajamas in 1955

Map Index

Tennessee
1 Davy Crockett Birthplace State Park
2 Rogersville
3 Cheek's Crossroads
4 Morristown
5 Dandridge
6 Knoxville
7 Murfreesboro
8 Lynchburg
9 Winchester
10 Maxwell
11 David Crockett State Park
12 Lawrenceburg
13 Centerville
14 Jackson
15 Trenton
16 Rutherford
17 Reelfoot Lake State Park
18 Memphis

Alabama
19 Huntsville
20 Ohatchee
21 Tallasehatchee
22 Talladega
23 Sylacauga
24 Tuscaloosa
25 Fort Mims

Florida
26 Pensacola

Arkansas
27 Little Rock
28 Washington

Texas
29 De Kalb
30 Jonesboro Crossing
31 Clarksville
32 Honey Grove
33 Acton
34 Nacagdoches
35 San Augustine
36 Crockett
37 Washington-on-the-Brazos State Historic Site
38 Bastrop
39 San Antonio

Selected Sites

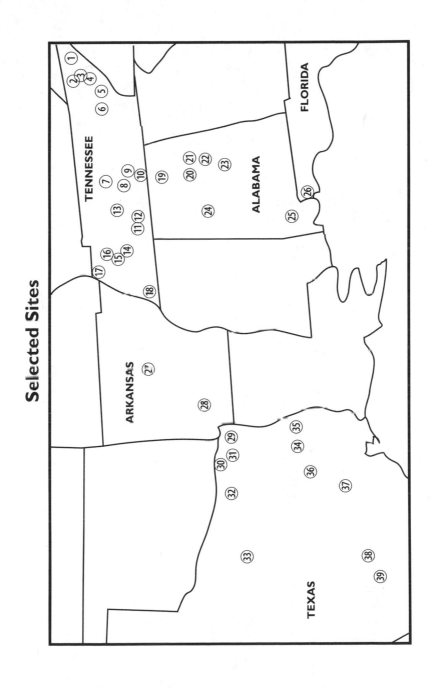

Map Index

North Carolina
1 Pleasant Gardens
2 Swannanoa
3 Fairview
4 Tuxedo

Virginia
5 Natural Bridge
6 Radford

West Virginia
7 Gerrardstown

District of Columbia
8 Washington

Maryland
9 Baltimore

Pennsylvania
10 Philadelphia

Selected Sites

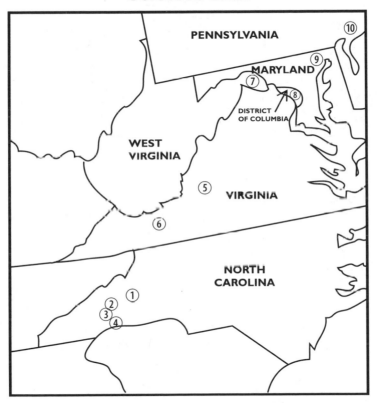

Contents

Preface   xv

Acknowledgments   xix

Introduction   xxiii

Tennessee	
Davy Crockett Birthplace State Park	1
Rogersville	8
Cheek's Crossroads	10
Morristown	13
Dandridge	20
Knoxville	28
Murfreesboro	29
Lynchburg	37
Winchester	38
Maxwell	41
David Crockett State Park	47
Lawrenceburg	51
Centerville	54
Jackson	56
Trenton	62
Rutherford	65
Reelfoot Lake State Park	83
Memphis	87

Alabama

Huntsville	95
Ohatchee	100
Tallasehatchee	105
Talladega	109
Sylacauga	112
Tuscaloosa	115
Fort Mims	121

Florida

Pensacola	129

North Carolina

Pleasant Gardens	134
Swannanoa	136
Fairview	140
Tuxedo	142

Virginia

Natural Bridge	149
Radford	151

West Virginia

Gerrardstown	155

District of Columbia

Washington	157

Maryland

Baltimore	170

Pennsylvania
Philadelphia   180

Arkansas
Little Rock   185
Washington   190

Texas
De Kalb   192
Jonesboro Crossing   194
Clarksville   195
Honey Grove   200
Acton   201
Nacogdoches   202
San Augustine   209
Crockett   211
Washington-on-the-Brazos State Historic Site   212
Bastrop   216
San Antonio   218

Appendix: David Crockett Sites in Chronological Order 242
Bibliography   244
Index   246

Preface

In the Footsteps of Davy Crockett is a historically accurate account of the life of one of America's frontier heroes. It takes readers to places where Crockett is commemorated because he was there or to places that commemorate events in which he participated. By convention among scholars of Crockett's life, the nickname Davy is most often used as a reference to the mythologized, comic, super-human persona created by 19th-century publishers. However, this book is about David Crockett the historical figure.

Combining history with geography provides new opportunities for understanding and appreciating the scope of lives lived in centuries past. But changes in terms and place names over the years can create confusion. I have therefore used modern terms and the modern names of communities. For the record, however, David Crockett went to Murfreesborough, not Murfreesboro. He went to Washington City, not Washington, D.C. He and all the volunteers fighting for Texas independence went to Béxar, not San Antonio. In fact, Texas was at the time of the 1836 revolution called Tejas. The native-born residents there were known as Tejanos. The colonists coming in from the United States and other countries were called Texians. In general, this book uses the familiar term *Texans* for both Anglo and Mexican residents of Tejas.

This book takes readers to 49 sites spread across 10 states plus the District of Columbia. There, they will find historical markers, plaques, monuments, statues, replica cabins, museums, shrines, and historic buildings commemorating Crockett's life. I have been to all the sites except two: the Second United States Bank in Philadelphia and Elizabeth Crockett Acton State Historic Site in Acton, Texas. I took all the photographs except three, as credited. In some cases, historical markers were missing at the time of my visit. Some are scheduled to be replaced. Vandalism, car accidents, and road construction could yet affect the presence of other markers.

It should be noted that Crockett's story involves four communities named Washington. The nation's capital is referred to as Washington, D.C. Washington and Old Washington refer to the town in southwest Arkansas. A third Washington, in Texas, was called such until after the Civil War, when it became known as Washington-on-the-Brazos. As a runaway youth of 13, Crockett also passed through Washington, Rappahannock County, Virginia.

David Crockett was not highly educated. His speech was colorful, his grammar uncertain, and his spelling creative. Much of what is read today as Crockett's accounts was edited by his contemporaries, who wanted to make him credible. When his personal accounts are quoted in this book, the errors are usually so obvious that I have avoided the use of *sic* to indicate the reproduction of grammatical errors from the original.

The release of this book in 2006 marks the 170th anniversary of Crockett's death at the Alamo on March 6, 1836. Crockett was a controversial national celebrity in his own lifetime, but he was not elevated to hero status until after his death. From that point, he became a martyr to Texas independence and a member of the pantheon of American folk heroes. This book's release also coincides with the 220th anniversary of Crockett's birth on August 19, 1786, at Limestone Creek, Greene County, Tennessee, and the 200th anniversary of his marriage on August 14, 1806, to Polly Finley near Dandridge, Tennessee. In a remarkable coincidence, David Crockett and Polly Finley were married on the 50th anniversary of the marriage of Daniel Boone and Rebecca Bryan on August 14, 1756. David and Polly were married in Jefferson County, Tennessee, and Daniel and Rebecca in what is now Davie County, North Carolina.

History does not record Crockett's ever wearing a coonskin cap until after he was parodied by an actor beginning in 1831. Even then, the accounts appeared only in a few reports written decades afterward about the final expedition of his life—his trip to Texas in the winter of 1835-36.

More than a half-century ago, James Atkins Shackford pursued the facts of David Crockett's life for his doctoral dissertation at Vanderbilt University. From that research, he wrote *David Crockett: The Man and the Legend*, which was published at the height of the Disney-inspired Crockett craze of the mid-1950s. As a published author, Shackford discovered what Crockett had learned 120 years earlier on the Tennessee campaign trail: people don't want to be informed, they want to be entertained. Hence, Disney's semifictional Davy prevailed in popularity over Shackford's carefully researched David. Still, for Crockett scholars, Shackford's work, with its extensive research notes and appendices, stands as the basis for any serious treatment of Crockett's life, including this one.

In the Footsteps of Davy Crockett covers the nearly 50 years of Crockett's life. It does not describe every site he visited. However, it does include the ones that offer an opportunity to connect with the episodes of his life that are of interest to most people.

If you have a site that you would like to see included, please contact me through www.blairpub.com, the website of John F. Blair, Publisher.

I have not attempted to interpret the life of David Crockett, as some others have seemed eager to do. As readers will discover in this book, Crockett was a complex man whose character, motives, and behavior may be challenging to understand 200 years later. Instead, I tell his life story by putting readers where Crockett was during the varied episodes of his life. Crockett was a product of a nation in transition between the American Revolution and the Civil War. The country was seeking to know its own direction in those years, and so was each citizen. Given that setting, this book offers readers the opportunity to discern for themselves from the accounts presented and from their own explorations in his footsteps the true character of celebrated American frontier hero David Crockett.

Acknowledgments

I received help from many people during my research. The book presented here is better than it might have been because of their contributions.

My mention of the persons listed below implies no responsibility on their part for any errors in this book. Any mistakes are mine and mine alone.

I thank:

Robert Goodson, for his help in locating the site of the Robert Patton Meeting House in Swannanoa, North Carolina

Bob Jarnagin, for his help in confirming the general location of the William Finley property in Jefferson County, Tennessee, and for mentioning the Finley Cemetery and the William Finley marker on private property

Joe Bone, manager at the Last Home of Davy Crockett Museum in Rutherford, Tennessee, for playing "The Crockett Victory March" on his harmonica

Joy Bland, historian for Direct Descendants and Kin of David Crockett, for sharing the documented genealogy of David Crockett's siblings

Anne Swann, director of the Historic Carson House in Pleasant Gardens, North Carolina, for providing a copy of the historical research report by Michael R. Hill on the history of the home and family

Rebecca Heath, library assistant at the Historical Society of Washington, D.C., for locating the site of Mrs. Ball's Boarding House

Raneé Pruitt, archivist in the Alabama Room at the Huntsville Public Library, for researching the location of Beaty's Spring (now called Brahan Springs)

Joe Swann, co-owner of the Crockett rifle on display at the East Tennessee Historical Society, for information about the documentation of this artifact

Cherel Henderson, director, and Michelle MacDonald, curator, of collections at the East Tennessee Historical Society, for information and photographs on the Crockett artifacts in the McClung Historical Collection

Texas Parks and Wildlife Department, for a photograph of the monument at Elizabeth Patton Crockett Acton State Historic Site

Karen Stevens, archivist at Independence National Historical Park, for help with a photo of the Second United States Bank

Bill Worthen, executive director of the Historic Arkansas Museum, for assistance in attempting to locate the site of the Jeffries Hotel

The staff of the Free Library of Philadelphia for providing newspaper accounts of Crockett's 1834 visit

Calhoun County commissioner James Eli Henderson and David

Pirritano, for help in locating the Tallasehatchee commemorative markers near Gadsden, Alabama

Jim Ezell of Tuscaloosa, Alabama, for his assistance in locating the probable site of Black Warrior Town as well as the previous site of the Black Warrior Town historic marker, since removed

My wife, Mary, for graciously accepting my diversion from family over the several months that I immersed myself in this project

My children and grandchildren, for reminding me there will always be a new generation eager for a good story

Carolyn Sakowski, Steve Kirk, and the rest of the staff at John F. Blair, Publisher, for championing this book and providing skillful, studied guidance during its creation

Other sources of help were:

The scholars and writers who uncovered the facts of David Crockett's life, most notably James Atkins Shackford, for his detailed biography, *David Crockett: The Man and the Legend*, the basis for all serious investigation into the life of this frontier personality

Mark Derr's 1993 book, *The Frontiersman: The Real Life and the Many Legends of Davy Crockett*, an exceptionally readable and well-informed exploration that added details beyond what Shackford provided and offered excellent documentation

Manley F. Cobia, Jr., who, in *Journey into the Land of Trials*, a scholarly examination of the "last chapter" in Crockett's life, explored newspaper articles and obscure personal accounts to divine the most probable set of activities and motivations that occupied Crockett from the time he left his home in West Tennessee on November 1, 1835, until he was killed at the Alamo four months and five days later

Richard Bruce Winders, historian and curator of the Alamo, who wrote authoritatively in *Sacrificed at the Alamo* about the political turmoil that doomed the volunteers to defeat

William Groneman III, a longtime student of the Alamo and the controversies that surround Crockett's demise, whose 2005 book, *David Crockett, Hero of the Common Man*, delved deeply into that episode of Crockett's life

And of course, Crockett's own *Narrative of the Life of David Crockett of the State of Tennessee* provided the colorful language and phrases and the personal perspective to enliven the telling of his story

Lastly, I also want to recognize my great-great-great-grandfather who followed in David Crockett's footsteps while they were both alive. Branch Jones (1775-c. 1845) was born on the bank of the Nolichucky River, served during the Creek War near Fort Mims, and was hunting and farming in St. Francis, Arkansas, when Crockett rode by on his way to the Alamo. My desire to know what his life was like put me on the path to discovering my own American heritage.

Introduction

As much as any culture, America loves its heroes. They tell us something about ourselves, what we admire, and to what we aspire. Our heroes remind us of our history and tell us something about the character of our society.

Children of the 1950s know Davy Crockett as an American hero, the "king of the wild frontier." They may think they know the man. Was he "alligator, half-man, half-horse," as was often said of him in the early 19th century? Could he "jump higher, squat lower, dive deeper, [and] come up drier than any other fellow in the country," as the first *Crockett Almanac* proclaimed in 1835? Could he really grin a bear down from a tree? Did he ever try?

The image of the famous Tennessee frontiersman that prevails in the imaginations of most Americans today is that fashioned by Walt Disney 50 years ago and expanded during the ensuing Crockett craze. Unfortunately, that image is mostly wrong and certainly incomplete.

For starters, the man was always known as David. Of course, Crockett did fight in the Creek War, serve in Congress, and die at the Alamo. That much Disney got right. But a host of other episodes from his life took him from Tennessee not only to Alabama,

Florida, Washington, D.C., and Texas, but to North Carolina, Virginia, Maryland, and Arkansas as well. In what seems antithetical to his frontiersman image, Crockett traveled to Baltimore, Philadelphia, New York, and Boston. At 39, he rafted down the Mississippi River headed for New Orleans on a business venture but almost drowned in the chaos of a shipwreck. Nearly a decade later, he steamed down the Ohio River making political speeches and immersing himself in the adulation of cheering crowds. As a boy of 12, he walked a well-worn wagon road, driving cattle to market. Some 30 years later, he experienced the newest development in transportation technology as he rode behind a steam-powered locomotive in the earliest days of railroading. Crockett's America was changing rapidly and expanding westward in leaps and bounds. He was changing with it.

The true story of David Crockett is one of image building. As much as any politician, he wanted people to think of him in a certain way. He wrote his own life's story to promote that image for a campaign to become president of the United States. He wrote about his poor and difficult childhood, his courtships and marriages, his volunteer service in the Creek War, and his bear-hunting exploits in West Tennessee. In addition, Crockett shared some painful and disquieting aspects of his personal life. He wrote about his failure to get a good education, the fearful relationship he had with his father, and the loss of his young spouse. He shared stories of the destruction of his distillery and gunpowder enterprise, his lifelong struggle with financial problems, and the insecurity he felt in his early service as an elected representative, which earned him the questionable sobriquet "gentleman from the cane."

Crockett was a bear hunter, a marksman, a scout, and a volunteer soldier. He was a son, a brother, a husband, and a father. He was a militia leader, a state legislator, and a United States congressman. He was an author, a farmer, and an entrepreneur. Crockett was his own man in Congress but also, perhaps unwittingly, a pawn of other politicians. He roundly criticized a sitting president and thought he would make a better one himself. But done with politics at age 49, he rode off to Texas looking to create the fortune that had eluded him thus far. Along the way, he got involved with the ambitions of American settlers on a new frontier to live freely and independently. Arriving in Texas a celebrity, he was perhaps initially uncertain of his own intentions. But in the end, he decided to follow his own famous advice: "Be always sure you are right, then go ahead." Crockett died a hero of the Texas Revolution and is revered today for his ultimate sacrifice.

Even before he died but certainly afterward, Crockett's celebrated persona was usurped by others and molded for their purposes. They attached to his name exaggerations, gross misrepresentations, and outright lies. In that way, the myth of Davy Crockett became a marketing sensation of the 19th century. He became "the wild man of the West." *The Lion of the West*, a stage farce by James Kirke Paulding, helped popularize the backwoods image of Crockett beginning in 1831. An unauthorized and sensational biography in 1833 and then Crockett's own publishing effort the following year to correct that false image further impressed on Americans the character of the colorful Tennessee congressman. *The Crockett Victory March*, published in 1835, furthered his celebrity before he lost his seat in Congress. The *Crockett Almanac*s were issued by various publishers from 1835 to 1856; these comic, fantasy publications kept the name, if not the truth, of the man in front of Americans for 20 years after he died. In 1872, Frank Mayo began portraying Crockett on stage in *Davy Crockett: Or Be Sure You're Right, Then Go Ahead*. Mayo performed the lead role for 24 years for audiences in America and England until his death in 1896. These interpretations, based on both fact and fiction, presided until movies furthered the Davy Crockett legend in the 20th century. In 1955, Disney trumped all prior efforts to market the name and image.

In the Footsteps of Davy Crockett is about the real life of the real man who lived from 1786 to 1836. It puts Crockett's life on the landscape and enables those who appreciate American history and heritage to touch his life across the centuries by following his footsteps. Readers can visit the sites where Crockett's life is commemorated and stand in the same spots where he hunted, fought, farmed, courted, campaigned, legislated, and eventually died. They can visit museums, view artifacts, and contemplate his life—one lived in such a manner that, two centuries later, Americans are still intrigued by David Crockett, "the wild man of the West," "the gentleman from the cane," the hero of the Alamo, and still today America's favorite frontier hero.

The replica cabin displays typical frontier furnishings and fare.

Davy Crockett Birthplace State Park

Davy Crockett Birthplace State Park lies near Limestone and the Greene County-Washington County line in East Tennessee, about 11 miles northeast of Greeneville off US 11E. From the turnoff, the park is 3.4 miles along Davy Crockett Road. It is also 12 miles southwest of Jonesborough, the oldest town in Tennessee and the site of the first capital of the failed State of Franklin.

A furnished replica cabin and an engraved steppingstone from the original cabin can be seen at the park. Limestone Creek and the Nolichucky River flow adjacent to the park, a popular site for RV campers. A walking trail leads to a waterfall. A small *museum at the visitor center includes displays about Crockett's life and the Disney Crockett craze of the 1950s; the museum may be closed on weekends. A monument erected by the Ruritans in 1965 includes a representation of all the states. It replaced the original commemorative monument erected in 1890.*

This home site at the confluence of Limestone Creek and the Nolichucky River is where David Crockett was born and spent his first few years.

David Crockett was most certainly not "born on a mountain top," as a popular song of the 1950s declared. Surprising to some, neither was he born in Tennessee, which the same Disney ballad also claimed. David Crockett was born in a time of turmoil, when the young United States was still struggling to establish itself as a constitutional government. As a result, the jurisdiction of his birth was in question, though its geography was certain. David Crockett was born along the banks of the Nolichucky River, a site that was by some accounts in North Carolina and by others in the State of Franklin.

Some writers say that the State of Franklin, proposed in the 1780s, was originally called Frankland. In German, it meant "land of freedom." The name was changed to Franklin to honor Benjamin Franklin in the hope of encouraging his support for its establishment. In fact, he was noncommittal.

The overmountain region where David's parents, John and Rebecca Crockett, settled in 1780 was isolated. The settlers in the valleys of the Nolichucky, Watauga, and Holston rivers had suffered from lack of government support for decades. Indeed, in 1772, settlers at Fort Watauga on the Holston River convened and established the first independent self-government in America, creating the Watauga Association. After the American Revolution, the settlers continued to feel slighted by North Carolina, though they sent elected representatives to the legislature convened in Hillsborough.

In 1784, when the opportunity for change presented itself, some in the region pursued it. That June, to pay for its portion of the debt incurred during the American Revolution, the North Carolina legislature, acting from Hillsborough, ceded to the federal government, operating under the Articles of Confederation, its lands west of the Alleghenies and reaching to the Mississippi River. North Carolina closed its land office in Jonesborough. The next month, the state withdrew the offer. However, many citizens of the overmountain region, having experienced inattention from North Carolina previously, decided they favored being under federal jurisdiction. Representatives of the citizens of four counties—Washington, Greene, Sullivan, and Davidson— convened that summer to create an independent government. By November 1785, they drafted a constitution. John Sevier was elected president, and the legislators met in session that same year in Jonesborough.

Unfortunately, North Carolina had already passed legislation

Views of the Nolichucky River are accessible along hiking trails in the park.

by which it claimed to retain administrative control over the area. Thus, for some time, two rival governments claimed authority in the overmountain region. John Sevier was the leader of the independent faction, commanding its militia and administration. John Tipton represented the interests of North Carolina. In the midst of this conflict and confusion, David Crockett was born in August 1786.

Before Crockett was three, the State of Franklin failed. The circumstances surrounding its demise illustrate the rough-and-tumble frontier life of the area. John Sevier had personally attacked political rival John Tipton with a cane; Tipton retaliated using his fists. Sevier's property was attached by North Carolina. Backed by a party of 150 militia, Sevier put Tipton's house under siege and engaged in a shooting battle. After warrants were issued against Sevier for atrocities committed by others against the Cherokees, Tipton chased down Sevier and arrested him. Sevier was taken in shackles to Morganton, North Carolina, where he was jailed. He escaped through a window at his trial and rode away. Later, when Tennessee became a state in 1796, John Sevier served as its first governor. Such was life on the frontier—of North Carolina or Franklin or Tennessee—during the days when David Crockett was a child.

John Crockett had lived in the overmountain region of what is now Tennessee since arriving in 1775 with his parents and brothers. In 1780, during the American Revolution, he rode with the Overmountain Men across the Appalachians in pursuit of Major Patrick Ferguson, whom they surrounded and defeated decisively at the Battle of Kings Mountain. John Crockett rode on that historic campaign as a militiaman under Colonel John Sevier.

In that same year, 1780, John Crockett married Rebecca (or Rebekah) Hawkins, whose family had moved to the overmountain area from Joppa, Maryland. John Crockett may have lived near

Joppa as well before moving to North Carolina around 1771. John's father was named David. That David Crockett family lived near what is now Beattie's Ford in east Lincoln County, North Carolina, from 1771 to 1775.

Some accounts claim that Rebecca Hawkins was a sister to John Sevier's first wife, Sarah. That would have made Colonel John Sevier an uncle by marriage to John and Rebecca's son David. Though Crockett biographer James Atkins Shackford claims this as fact, it is curious that someone as politically motivated as David Crockett did not make use of such a connection to Tennessee's first governor and one of the region's most powerful and influential leaders. For that reason, many historians discount the suggested family connection.

After marrying Rebecca, John Crockett purchased land for a homestead in Washington County, North Carolina. It was located within a larger parcel known as (Jacob) Brown's Purchase. When Greene County was formed from Washington, Crockett's home was included in Greene. In April 1783, Crockett became constable. He also served as constable in 1785 and 1789 and probably when the area was under the jurisdiction of the State of Franklin.

As settlers flowed into the region during those early years, the inhabitants could make money by speculating in land. In October 1783, John Crockett purchased 200 acres in Sullivan County for 100 shillings. In June 1787, less than four years later, he and Rebecca, both signing their names to the sale rather than "making their mark," sold it for 50 pounds.

Before 1786, John Crockett purchased land along Limestone Creek where it flows into the Nolichucky River. In the cabin John built on that property, Rebecca gave birth to a sixth child on August 17, 1786. They named him David after his paternal grandfather. Though the name of the oldest child is unknown, and perhaps was a daughter who died young, according to documented records of the Direct Descendants and Kin of David Crockett, David's older brothers were Nathan, William, Aaron, and James Patterson. David had a younger brother, John, followed by two sisters—Elizabeth (called Betsy) and Rebecca.

David Crockett shared in his autobiography only a few recollections from his childhood, but they were certainly memorable.

One event occurred at the Limestone Creek cabin site. In the days when he was so young that, as he declared, "I had no knowledge of the use of breeches," Crockett witnessed the rescue of his brothers from going over a waterfall. His four older brothers and a neighbor boy named Campbell, then nearly grown at age 15, took John Crockett's canoe into the Nolichucky River. Though the Crockett boys knew how to handle a canoe quite well, Campbell would not relinquish the paddle. In short order, the boys were adrift and headed stern-first toward the falls, which dropped straight down. Crockett recalled that Amos Kendall was working in his fields and saw what was about to happen. He came running, Crockett said, "like a cane brake afire," tearing off his coat, jacket, and shirt as he came. "I had no doubt," recalled Crockett, "but the devil or something else was after him." Kendall jumped into the river in his breeches. He swam when he had to and waded when he could touch the bottom until he managed to grab the canoe. He pulled long and hard to stop it, then started hauling it upstream against the current. After a time, Kendall pulled the boys to safety. They got out, still frightened. Crockett judged the episode to be "a punishment on them for leaving me on shore."

On another occasion, after the Crocketts had moved to a different farm, young David witnessed his father tend to a man, Absalom Stonecipher, who had been accidentally shot. Joseph

Hawkins, the brother of Rebecca Hawkins Crockett, was hunting one day when he mistook Stonecipher, who was picking grapes, for a deer. Stonecipher was carried to the nearby home of Samuel Humbert, after which David's father passed a silk handkerchief completely through the wound, which was believed to clean it. David was amazed enough to recall the incident over 40 years later in his autobiography. Stonecipher recovered and later married Humbert's daughter, Sarah.

Looking for ways to improve his life and livelihood, John Crockett attempted other enterprises, trying his hand first at milling and then at tavern keeping (see the section on Morristown, pages 13-20).

A commemorative monument and a replica of the John Crockett cabin sit along the Nolichucky River.

Rogersville

Rogersville is near the center of Hawkins County in East Tennessee at the intersection of US 11W and TN 66. From the post office on Main Street (Old US 11W) at Hasson Road in Rogersville, go south two blocks to Rogan Road. A historic marker there notes the Rogers Cemetery a quarter-mile east in David Crockett Park. The walled cemetery at the park contains several grave markers and a bronze plaque erected in 1927 by the Tennessee Department of History. The plaque commemorates the 1777 attack and murder of David Crockett (the grandfather) and his wife, whose name is unknown.

In 1776, the settlers of the overmountain region of North Carolina (today part of Tennessee) negotiated a treaty with the Cherokees. Together, they crafted the Long Island Treaty, which was to bring about the cessation of hostilities that had overrun the area as more settlers came over the mountains. Despite the treaty's provisions and assurances, land speculators soon laid claim to over a million acres clearly reserved for the Indian population. Dragging Canoe broke with his Cherokee chieftain father and led a renegade group of Cherokees and Creeks who became know as the Chickamaugas. They attacked frequently and ferociously the settlers who were intruding on their Cherokee homelands. During that time, attacks against colonial settlers by the Cherokees were also encouraged by British agents who were prosecuting a war against the Patriots.

In 1777, David Crockett's grandparents were among 12 people massacred by a marauding band of Cherokee and Creek warriors. The Crocketts were killed at their homestead. John Crockett, father of the famous frontiersman, was away patrolling the area as a ranger in the militia. However, two of John's brothers, Joseph and James, were attacked at home. Joseph was wounded in the fight, suffering a broken arm from a musket ball. James, deaf and mute from birth, was captured. He remained a captive of the Cherokees for 17 years and nine months, when he was rescued after his brothers learned he was still alive. They paid a ransom to an Indian trader who secured James's release. "Deaf and Dumb Jimmy," as he was known to his family, returned to the settlements but spent the rest of his life trying to find the silver mines he had been taken to while a captive. Unfortunately, he had been blindfolded every time. Indeed, tales of the John Swift Silver Mines and of Cherokee treasure secreted in mountain caves had captured the interest of frontiersmen and treasure seekers since the mid-1700s. Some believe Daniel Boone spent time during 1771 in the Virginia mountains around Pound Gap hunting for the rumored treasure.

During this period of conflict on the frontier, the settlers in

The grandfather for whom David Crockett was named is buried near the site where he and his wife were killed by Indians in 1777.

the overmountain region along the Watauga, Holston, and Nolichucky rivers were attempting to govern themselves. They had formed the Watauga Association in 1772 as the first independent government in America. Though the boundary between Virginia and North Carolina had been surveyed in 1728-29, it had not been extended as far west as the overmountain region. Many of the predominantly Scots-Irish settlers had moved into the area by following the Holston Valley south. Most were Virginians and believed they were still in Virginia. As the Indian attacks increased, the overmountain settlers petitioned both North Carolina and Virginia in July 1776 to be annexed and protected. David Crockett (the grandfather) and his son William signed the petition to North Carolina. David also signed the petition to Virginia, as did his son John, future father of the frontiersman. By mid-1777, North Carolina took control of the area and established two counties—Washington and Sullivan.

Sycamore Shoals State Historic Site in Elizabethton, Tennessee, commemorates the history of early settlers along the Watauga River, including their effort at self-government.

Cheek's Crossroads

Three miles northeast of Morristown in Hamblen County, Old Kentucky Road crosses US 11E/TN 34. A historic marker at Cheek's Crossroads indicates the nearby site of the Jesse Cheek store. Farther northeast, US 11E parallels the old stage road toward Greeneville. A historic marker along this route from Russellville to Bulls Gap was missing at the time of this writing. It read, "Old Stage Road—This road was an important artery of transportation between Washington and the western frontier. From Abingdon, Virginia, to White's Fort, later

Cheek's Crossroads was the starting point for the episode in young David's life when he ran away from home in fear of his father. His adventures over the next three years as a drover and laborer took him through the piedmont of Virginia, then to Baltimore, and eventually back home along the well-traveled Wilderness Road and the Abingdon-Knoxville Road.

In the fall of 1799, Crockett, then age 13, ran away from home at the Crockett Tavern to escape his angry father. David had not been attending classes for which his father was paying good money. Furthermore, he hid his truancy from his father. John Crockett became so enraged that he chased David, intending to thrash him, but David hid in the brush and escaped. Knowing that he could not return home at least for a while, he determined to leave. He walked a few miles to Jesse Cheek's store, where he hired himself out as a drover. One of his brothers, believed to have been John, went along, too.

The party of drovers started at Cheek's Crossroads and headed north into Virginia. Crockett recorded in his autobiography the towns through which they passed: "We set out and went on through Abbingdon, and the county seat of Withe county, in the State of Virginia; and then through Lynchburg, by Orange court-house, and Charlottesville, passing through what was called Chester Gap, on to a town called Front Royal." Though the names of some of the communities have changed over the years, the modern traveler might replicate Crockett's trek by following this route: Cheek's Crossroads, Greeneville, Jonesborough, Blountville, Bristol, Abingdon, Marion (Royal Oak), Wytheville (Evansham), Fort

Chiswell, Radford (Inglish Meadows), Christiansburg, Salem, Bedford (Liberty), New London, Lynchburg, New Glasgow, Charlottesville, Orange Court House, Madison, Washington, Chester Gap, and Front Royal.

After Crockett and his brother arrived at Front Royal, the cattle were sold. Crockett started back south, traveling with a brother of the man who had sold the cattle. His own brother was planning to follow later. After three days on the road, during which his traveling companion never offered to share the one horse they had, Crockett told the fellow he was heading on alone. The otherwise inconsiderate fellow traveler gave Crockett four dollars for his long trip home.

Shortly after starting out on his own, Crockett met a teamster named Adam Myers, whom he recalled as a being a "jolly good fellow." Myers was heading north from Greeneville, Tennessee. He told Crockett that after he reached Gerrardstown in what is now West Virginia, he would be returning home. Deciding to join him, Crockett got on the wagon and headed north. After two days, they met Crockett's brother on his own return trip. He tried to persuade Crockett to return home. Despite his brother's pleas, Crockett still feared his father's wrath. He continued with Myers to Gerrardstown as his brother continued south and home. Though Crockett never named this brother in his autobiography, others have claimed it was John.

In Gerrardstown, Myers was unable to find a return load immediately. He headed to Alexandria to try his luck there. Meanwhile, Crockett found light work, mostly plowing, with John Gray, who paid him 25 cents a day. Myers could only find work hauling goods to Baltimore, so he delayed his return trip to Tennessee. Crockett continued to work for Gray.

In the spring of 1800, Crockett took the money he had saved

and bought himself some better clothes. Afterward, he joined Myers on a trip to Baltimore so he could see the city. He gave the remainder of his savings—some seven dollars—to Myers for safekeeping. The trust Crockett placed in the man he had befriended was soon tested (see the section on Baltimore, Maryland, pages 170-74).

Morristown

Morristown is in the center of Hamblen County northeast of Knoxville. The Crockett Tavern Museum is on Morningside Drive 0.2 mile west of Haun Drive, which runs between US 11E (Andrew Johnson Highway) and East Morris Boulevard. Haun Drive is 0.3 mile west of the intersection of US 11E and US 25E. The Crockett Tavern Museum, dedicated in 1958, is operated by the Hamblen Chapter of the Association for the Preservation of Tennessee Antiquities. It is open seasonally from early May through late October. The state historic marker at the site was missing at the time of this writing. It read, "Crockett Tavern—Here stood the Crockett Tavern, established and operated by John and Rebecca Crockett, parents of David Crockett (1786-1836). It was the boyhood home of this pioneer and political leader of Tennessee who was later a victim of the Alamo Massacre at San Antonio, Texas."

The Crockett Tavern Museum is a replica cabin built on the site of the boyhood home of David Crockett. The original cabin survived into the Civil War, when it was used as a hospital for victims of smallpox. It was burned afterward to prevent the spread of the disease. Timbers from other local buildings, including Panther

Springs Academy, the John Cox house, and the 1823 Wolfe store-house, were used. The hinges on the front door came from Bent Creek Baptist Church, where Rebecca Crockett attended services. The artifacts and furniture in the museum, authentic to the period, offer an image of what life in a tavern and wagon-road ordinary (inn) were like.

In the early 1790s, John Crockett, David's father, was struggling financially as his family grew. He moved the family from place to place as he speculated in buying and then selling the land on which they lived. He was only marginally successful, if at all, in these ventures, so by 1794 he decided to try his hand at earning a living as a miller. Along with Thomas Galbraith (or Galbreath), he built a gristmill at the mouth of Cove Creek, a tributary of the Nolichucky River in southeast Greene County that flows into that river about two miles below the Nolichucky Dam, which creates Davy Crockett Lake. As the mill neared completion, a heavy rain came. The mill was washed away by what David, then seven or eight years old, later recalled as a "second epistle to Noah's

The Crockett Tavern Museum was built from logs taken from other period structures in the area.

fresh[et]." The water rose so high that it reached the cabin in which the family lived. Though David's own account was rather sparse on details, saying only that John Crockett moved the family members to prevent their drowning, fictional accounts written decades and centuries later for children's books have shown the family dramatically escaping the rapidly rising water as it swept the cabin away.

Following the loss of the mill, John Crockett was in debt. He needed a source of income and a place for his family to live. He moved them onto land they already owned. Records show that on April 14, 1792, before building the mill, John Crockett had bought 300 acres on Mossy Creek in Jefferson County. After losing the gristmill in the flood, the family moved to this Mossy Creek land. However, by November 1795, some or all of it was sold by the sheriff to settle a debt of $400. A bid of $40 gained the land but cleared the debt. The Crocketts continued to live on the land under some unknown arrangement, and John Crockett built an ordinary there for feeding and lodging travelers along the Knoxville-Abingdon Road. The clientele was most always wagoners, drovers, and teamsters. Men of those occupations were generally a rough group to have as guests in one's home, but John and Rebecca Crockett operated the enterprise with marginal success for the next couple of decades.

Due to the family's financial situation, it is not surprising that around 1798, John Crockett hired out David, then age 12, to Jacob Siler to help drive a herd of cattle to Rockbridge County, Virginia. As a drover, David was to walk with the cattle and keep them moving along the road. Rockbridge was 400 miles away. This was young David's first time away from his home and family. He was gone about seven months. (For more information, see the section on Natural Bridge, Virginia, pages 149-51.)

In the fall of the year after young David returned from his

cattle drive to Rockbridge, his father enrolled him in a local school run by Benjamin Kitchen. David and his brothers attended together. After just four days—which were enough for David "to learn my letters a little," he recalled—he got into a confrontation with another student, a larger and older boy. David sneaked out of the school, hid in the brush along the road, and waited for the other student. When the fellow came by, David sprang from the bushes and jumped on him. "I scratched his face all to a flitter jig," Crockett recalled, "and made him cry out for quarters in good earnest."

Fearful of the teacher's reprisals, David did not return to the school. Instead, he hid out in the woods each day and enlisted his brothers' help in keeping the secret of his absences from their father. In time, Kitchen wrote a note to John Crockett inquiring as to David's whereabouts. John confronted David with the note. "I knew very well I was in a devil of a hobble," Crockett recalled, "for my father had been taking a few horns, and was in a good condition to make the fur fly."

When David explained his fear of Kitchen and declared he would not return to school, his father became enraged. He broke off a thick hickory switch and started chasing the boy. "I put out with all my might," recalled Crockett, "and soon we were both up to the top of our speed. We had a tolerable tough race for about a mile." After young David crested a hill, he turned into the bushes and hid. He watched his father run past "puffing and blowing, as if his steam was enough to burst his boilers."

After his father gave up the chase, David walked to the nearby home of Jesse Cheek. While he was there, he and one of his brothers hired themselves on as drovers for a cattle drive into Virginia. David was running away from home. He was so afraid of his father that he was determined not to return. (For more information, see the sections on Cheek's Crossroads, pages 10-13; Gerrardstown,

West Virginia, pages 155-56; Baltimore, Maryland, pages 170-79; and Radford, Virginia, pages 151-54.)

Crockett spent about three years away from home. He worked as a drover and a laborer. He worked for a wagoner and a hatter. He plowed fields, saved money, and bought new clothes. He almost sailed for England as a cabin boy and almost drowned in a canoe crossing a river. He saw some new sights and fended for himself pretty well in a less-than-genteel world. Still, he longed to come back home.

Crockett had grown some in the years he was gone. When he returned, he was nearly six feet tall. No doubt, his appearance and voice had changed as well. Since his family had no expectation that they would ever see their David again, he was able to remain unidentified for a while. He hoped to remain so until he could determine what sort of reception he would receive.

When David arrived at the Crockett Tavern, several teamsters were already there, and the home was full of activity. He inquired if he could spend the night and was admitted. After a while, a meal was served. He sat at the table, not saying much. Whether it was by her recognition of his changed face or his display of some small but familiar mannerism at the table, Crockett's oldest sister, Betsy, realized who this stranger was. She jumped up, hugged David's neck, and declared, "Here is my lost brother."

A great commotion of joy and astonishment erupted at the table. Crockett wrote that he was so touched by the warmth of his family's embrace that he wished he had "submitted to a hundred whippings, sooner than cause so much affliction." He learned that his family had received no word of him at all since the time his brother had returned from the cattle drove. He also learned that his father was happy to see him return. Thus, he received no whipping for the prior offense.

The kitchen served travelers stopping at the John Crockett home and ordinary.

Crockett concluded his description of this episode from his life by declaring that though he was nearing manhood, he "did not know the first letter in the book." He remained an unschooled lad with an uncertain future.

In the weeks that followed, he learned that, during his absence, his father had become indebted to a neighbor named Abraham Wilson. John Crockett proposed to David that if he would work off that debt, he would release David from his responsibility to give his earnings to his father, as was the custom of the day. David agreed and set about working off the $36 debt. He labored six months without missing a day. At the end of that time, he was given his father's note. Wilson wanted Crockett to continue working for him and tried to hire him, but David thought better of it. "It was a place where a heap of bad company met to drink and gamble," he remembered. He did not want such a reputation.

Crockett next went to work for "an honest old Quaker," John Kennedy (or Canady). He paid Crockett two shillings a day on trial, then hired him after a week. It was then that he showed David a note for $40 he held on John Crockett. David agreed to work for six months if Kennedy would surrender the note. Kennedy agreed.

Deeds recorded in Jefferson County show that John Kennedy purchased several tracts of land in the area. The exact site of the Kennedy home where Crockett worked is not known. However, one location looks somewhat probable. In 1799, Kennedy purchased 194 acres "opposite to the head of Panther Creek" and adjacent to land described as "on the south side of the Holston River on the north side of the knobs that divide the waters of French Broad and Holston rivers." Today's Morristown Municipal Airport sits in an area that meets this general description. If this was the land on which Crockett worked, it was not distant from either the Crockett Tavern (perhaps seven miles) or the Finley home (some five miles), where Crockett later courted. But again, the actual site of the John Kennedy home is unknown at present.

After six months, during which Crockett never went to visit his parents, he was given the note and the loan of a horse by his employer. David rode home and handed the note to his father, who assumed Kennedy had sent it for collection. It was then that David explained that he had worked it off and was presenting it as a present to his father. Crockett recorded that his father "shed a heap of tears" and said he was sorry he had nothing to give David in return. Crockett may well have concluded that this exchange settled the matter with the father and that all personal debts were paid. He made no further mention of his father or their confrontational relationship in his autobiography.

Crockett returned to work for Kennedy. After having labored for a year to satisfy his father's debts, he was pleased to be working for himself, as he needed some new clothes. After about two months, Kennedy's young niece arrived from North Carolina, and Crockett fell in love for the first time. When he saw her, his heart would "flutter like a duck in a puddle" and his words would "get right smack up in my throat, and choke me like a cold potato." Eventually, he got up the nerve to tell her of his deep and abiding admiration. Though pleased with his attention, she informed him that she was engaged to marry her cousin, a son of John Kennedy. "I saw quick enough my cake was dough," Crockett said, "and I tried to cool off as fast as possible; but I had hardly safety pipes enough, as my love was so hot as mighty nigh to burst my boilers." He pursued the young woman no further.

At that point, Crockett decided that all his problems derived from his lack of education. He arranged with another of Kennedy's sons, who was a teacher, to instruct him four days a week and to let him work the other two for room and board. Crockett pursued his education in that manner for six months. "I learned to read a little in my primer," Crockett recalled, "to write my own name, and to cypher some in the first three rules in figures." He said he would have studied longer had he not decided that what he needed most of all was a wife (see the next section on Dandridge).

Dandridge

Dandridge is the county seat of Jefferson County. It sits along the French Broad River where TN 92 and TN 139 intersect. The Jefferson County Courthouse is on West Main Street at Gay Street. Museum displays, many relating to David Crockett, are exhibited throughout the first- and second-floor halls of the courthouse. They include a log from the chimney corner of the John Crockett cabin on Limestone Creek and a $10 note issued in January 1834 bearing an original signature by Crockett's political ally Nicholas Biddle, president of the Second United States Bank.

> *Finley Gap is in Jefferson County about six miles north of*
> *Dandridge, not far from the interchange of I-81 and I-40.*
> *From Colliers Corner (the intersection of Chucky Pike and*
> *Dumplin Valley Road), proceed half a mile southeast on Chucky*
> *Pike to the high point on the road and the intersection with*
> *Wheat Way. This is Finley Gap. The exact location of the Wil-*
> *liam Finley farm is unknown, but it was in this vicinity. A*
> *Finley family cemetery is on private property. The location of*
> *the rented farm where David and Polly Crockett first lived is*
> *unknown, but it is believed by some researchers to be perhaps*
> *a quarter-mile north and west of Colliers Corner, an area that*
> *remains undeveloped farmland.*

Dandridge is the town where the courtship history of young David Crockett is recorded. His accounts in his autobiography combined with the courthouse records tell a story of love found, lost, and found again. Dandridge, by the way, was named for Martha Dandridge, who became at her marriage Mrs. George Washington.

Dandridge was not exactly in the neighborhood of the John Kennedy farm, where Crockett lived and worked at that time, but for a man with courting and marriage on his mind, it was not too far away. Crockett recalled a family with several pretty daughters he had known when he was younger. He called on them and after a while focused his attentions on one who seemed interested. They attended the wedding of two Kennedy cousins, the bride having been Crockett's first love (see the previous section on Morristown). After that, the young woman Crockett was courting agreed to marry him.

About that time, Crockett made good friends with a fellow about his age who was an indentured servant of Kennedy. This fellow had his heart set on the affections of the sister of Crockett's

In 1844, the current Jefferson County Courthouse replaced the log structure at which David Crockett applied for two marriage licenses.

future bride. To pursue their courting without Kennedy's knowledge, the two young men would retire early to their upstairs beds, then climb out the window and down a pole they had leaned against the house. Wearing their Sunday clothes, they rode horseback 10 miles to Dandridge to court the young women, being sure to return before daybreak.

A few days before he was to marry the young woman, Crockett had still not informed her parents of his intentions. At that time, he learned of a shooting match and frolic to be held at a place that was on the way to his fiancée's house; James Atkins Shackford, Crockett's principal modern biographer, declared the date was Saturday, October 19, 1805. The prize was a beef divided, as was the practice, into quarters, to be awarded to the winners of various contests. Crockett's marksmanship was superb. He won the entire beef, including the "fifth quarter"—the hide, horns, and tallow. Selling it all for five dollars put him in a splendid mood.

Crockett proceeded to Dandridge on Monday to secure a li-

A log from the original John Crockett cabin stands in the courthouse's hallway museum.

cense for the marriage, which was to take place on Thursday. Afterward, he went to visit his fiancée but decided to stop first at her uncle's house to ask about the family. There, he found his fiancée's sister in a sad mood. Though she was reluctant to share what saddened her, when Crockett pressed her, she burst into tears and announced that her sister was marrying another the next day, and not David three days later as planned. This surprised Crockett like "a clap of thunder on a bright, sunny day," he said. "It struck me perfectly speechless for some time, and made me feel so weak that I thought I should sink down." Though assured by the sister that he could break up the match if he pursued it, he decided against trying. Crockett wrote, "My heart was so bruised, and my spirits were broken down; so I bid her farewell, and turned my lonesome and miserable steps back again homeward, concluding that I was only born for hardships, misery, and disappointments."

Though Crockett did not mention by name in his autobiography the woman who jilted him, her name appeared on the wedding license he had secured at the Jefferson County Courthouse on October 21, 1805. She was Margaret Elder. Moreover, Crockett's account of the incident may not have told the full story. James Shackford suggested that Crockett's appetite for such community frolics as the shooting match probably ran to excess. Perhaps stories of his drinking, dancing, and carousing with other girls reached the home of his fiancée before he did. It might have been that Crockett's reluctance to call on his fiancée and her parents to press for her hand was due to his feelings of guilt. No one alive knows for sure, so history is left with only Crockett's account and a healthy speculation about the truth.

In the fall of 1805, Crockett despaired for "a good long time," by his account, over losing the affections of Miss Elder. Eventually, he began to look for other marriage prospects. He stopped at the home of a Dutch widow who had a daughter who was, he said, "well enough as to smartness, but she was as ugly as a stone fence." She must have had a kind heart, because upon seeing Crockett's dejected nature, she promised that she would introduce him to a "pretty little girl" if he would come to the reaping soon to be held. He agreed.

Although John Kennedy counseled him against going because of the effect such bad company could have on his reputation, he did attend as planned. The Dutch girl introduced him first to a talkative Irish matron who was, in fact, mother to the pretty little girl. As Crockett recalled it after he later was introduced to the girl, "I must confess I was plaguy [excessively] well pleased with her from the word go. She had a good countenance, and was very pretty, and I was full bent on making up an acquaintance with her." They danced a reel, talked, and played games into the early hours. Crockett was delighted with his prospects for finding happiness after meeting this young woman. Since he had to deal with the expectations of the mother as well, he spent some time talking to her. Crockett called it "salting the cow to catch the calf."

Crockett returned to work, having made a bargain to labor six months for one of the Kennedys for a horse. After six weeks, he went to visit the girl and again met her parents, whom he described as "a very clever old man, and the woman as talkative as ever." While he was there, the pretty little girl returned home in the company of another suitor. Crockett decided to hold firm to his own suit. In the course of the evening, she expressed to Crockett her interest in him. The other fellow sat across the room gritting his teeth, Crockett looking at him every now and again "as fierce as a wildcat," he wrote. Unfortunately, the mother was set on the other suitor and made Crockett's courting difficult. Fortunately, the pretty little girl liked him best.

About two weeks later, Crockett joined in a wolf hunt with several men and their dogs. They chose a sparsely inhabited area that was unfamiliar to Crockett. While he was hunting, the sky darkened as a storm rolled in. Soon, he found that he had no idea which way was back to his comrades. He chose a course and set out for six miles or so, but it proved to be the wrong direction. As evening was overtaking him, he spied a woman walking through the woods. He followed her in the fading light and caught up with her at last. They were both surprised; it was his pretty little girl. She had been chasing her father's horses, she said, and was now lost in the woods herself. "She had been traveling all day and was mighty tired," Crockett recalled. "I thought she looked sweeter than sugar." They walked on together and found a path that led them to an empty cabin just as darkness fell. They stayed in the cabin together. By Crockett's account, "I sat up all night courting." In the morning, they went their separate ways, she seven miles to home and he some 10.

Regardless of what modern readers may imagine happened in

this historic encounter or wonder at how two young people so in-fatuated with each other came to be at the same isolated, distant cabin just at dusk, previous generations have interpreted it inno-cently or even heroically. Mark Derr pointed out in his book *The Frontiersman* that this incident was portrayed over 2,000 times from 1874 to 1896 in the Frank Mayo theatrical production *Davy Crockett: Or Be Sure You're Right, Then Go Ahead.* In that production, Crockett stood all night with his arm stretched across the door, bracing it against the relentless attack of hungry wolves that repeatedly leaped against it. By his actions, Crockett protected both the life and the virtue of the object of his affections. This scene was repeated later in silent movies inspired by the play. This same heroic deed has been portrayed in children's books and juvenile literature as well. It became part of the legend of Davy Crockett.

Crockett subsequently returned to work and went to see the pretty little girl from time to time. Eager to marry her, he was finally able to buy the horse from teacher Kennedy by throwing his rifle into the bargain. Astride his mount, he rode to see his fiancée to set the date for the wedding. He was not welcomed by her mother. "She looked at me," Crockett wrote, "as savage as a meat axe." He tried to reason with her about the proposed mar-riage, but "her Irish was up too high to do anything with her." He rode off, declaring that he would come the following Thursday with a horse and bridle to fetch his fiancée. On his ride home, he ar-ranged with a justice of the peace to marry them.

On August 14, 1806, Crockett was determined to marry the pretty little girl in spite of her mother's opposition. He started toward the farm of the girl's family on Thursday as promised with quite an entourage of friends and family. Two miles from the house, the party came upon a large gathering of people who had heard there was to be a wedding. Crockett sent his best man ahead. He returned soon enough, the father of Crockett's fiancée having filled his bottle; they were welcomed to approach. Crockett rode into the yard and without dismounting bade his bride to mount the horse he was leading and to depart with him. As they rode away, they reached the gate where the father was standing. He entreated Crockett to stay and marry there, declaring that he was agreeable to the match but admitting that, as Crockett described it, "his wife, like most women, had entirely too much tongue." Crockett agreed to stay if his future mother-in-law would apologize. She did so reluctantly, explaining that this was her first child to marry. Crockett and his fiancée remained at her family's farm and married. "We had as good treatment as could be expected, and that night all went on well," Crockett declared, briefly summarizing the wedding night.

In the morning, they rode to his parents' home, where a large party of visitors celebrated with the newlyweds. "Having gotten my wife, I thought I was completely made up, and needed nothing more in the whole world," Crockett recalled. "But I soon found this was all a big mistake—for now having a wife, I wanted everything else; and, worse than all, I had nothing to give for it."

To this point in his autobiography, Crockett never mentioned the name of the pretty little girl. But the records of Jefferson County in the courthouse in Dandridge show that he applied for a marriage license on August 12, 1806, to Mary Finley, who was called Polly. The wedding was two days later, just three days before Crockett turned 20. Her parents were William and Jean Finley (or Finlay). The bond for $1,250, payable should he fail to marry the girl, was signed by Crockett's friend Thomas Doggett.

Crockett rented a small cabin and farm near Polly's parents. His in-laws gave them a cow and calf for a marriage dowry. John Kennedy gave David and Polly an account at a store for $15 so they could buy things they needed to set up a home. The couple then set about making their way on their own. David hunted and farmed. Polly was skilled with spinning and weaving. After a while, Crockett despaired of getting ahead. "In this time, we had two sons," he recalled, "and I found I was better at increasing my family than my fortune."

The Crocketts decided to find a new land where they would not have to rent and where the hunting might be better. They chose an area that people were just starting to settle, the Duck River and Elk River country in south-central Tennessee. (For more information, see the section on Lynchburg, pages 37-38.)

Knoxville

Knoxville is located in east-central Tennessee where I-40 and I-75 cross. The East Tennessee Historical Society Museum, at 601 South Gay Street, was renovated in 2005. Home to the McClung Historical Collection, it offers extensive exhibits about the people and cultures of the earliest communities in the state. The East Tennessee Historical Society was founded in 1834.

Although no visit by David Crockett to Knoxville is prominent in the records, his presence is strong today at the East Tennessee Historical Society Museum. The McClung Historical Collection exhibits the powder horn of Absalom Stonecipher. Mistaken for a deer in foliage, he was shot accidentally by Crockett's uncle Joseph Hawkins while he was hunting. Also displayed is the family Bible of Samuel Humbert, at whose home young David witnessed his fa-

David Crockett's first rifle is on display at the East Tennessee Historical Society Museum.
COURTESY OF EAST TENNESSEE HISTORICAL SOCIETY

ther clean Stonecipher's wound with a silk handkerchief (see the section on Davy Crockett Birthplace State Park, pages).

Crockett's first rifle is also exhibited. He bought it in 1803 but in 1806 traded it and three months' labor for a "courting horse" so he could pursue Polly Finley, who became his first wife. The rifle is on loan from descendants of James McCuistion, who probably purchased it from a son of John Kennedy (or Canady), who owned the horse. The rifle was previously displayed in Nashville at the Tennessee State Museum from 1982 to 1995 (see the section on Dandridge, page 7).

Murfreesboro

Murfreesboro (spelled Murfreesborough in the 1820s), the county seat of Rutherford County, sits at the intersection of US 231 and US 41 adjacent to I-24 about 30 miles southeast of Nashville. It was the state capital from June 1, 1818, through April 30, 1826, as is commemorated by a monument on the southwest corner of the courthouse square, located at Maple and Main streets. The courthouse is one of only six in Tennessee dating from before the Civil War.

Cannonsburgh Village, a bicentennial project begun in 1974, is a living-history museum that commemorates early life in

*the South through the interpretive display of historic build-
ings including a one-room school, a general store, a gristmill,
and other structures. It is located at 312 South Front Street,
one block south of Broad Street (US 41).*

*First Presbyterian Church was the site where the Tennessee
General Assembly met in 1822. Two historic markers for the
church are on East Vine Street between South Academy Street
and East Maney Avenue, three blocks east and one block south
of the courthouse.*

David Crockett is remembered today as a celebrated bear
hunter and frontiersman of the 19th century and as a martyr of the
Texas Revolution. During his lifetime, his national notoriety arose
from the personal eccentricities he displayed during his political
career as a United States congressman. That service followed his
tenure as a state legislator in two general assemblies in Tennessee,
from the fall of 1821 through the summer of 1825. He served in
Murfreesboro, which became the state capital in 1818.

On September 17, 1821, Crockett joined the other representatives from across Tennessee in Murfreesboro for the convening of
the 14th General Assembly. During his first session, he demon
strated his interest in one particular issue that would dominate his
political life. He was concerned about the administration of the
West Tennessee lands. This issue had its roots in North Carolina
and involved the satisfaction of land warrants issued by that state
for service to the Patriot cause during the American Revolution by
persons such as Crockett's father-in-law, Robert Patton. It also involved North Carolina's efforts to shed itself of the lands that became the State of Franklin and ultimately Tennessee. Moreover,
this matter affected Crockett's personal prospects and immediate
future as well.

*Cannonsburgh Village presents historic
buildings for interpreting frontier life.*

North Carolina had issued land grants for service in the American Revolution but had done a poor job of accounting for how much land was granted and how many warrants were issued. The state offered its western lands (i.e., Tennessee) to the federal government as long as it would honor the land grants issued by North Carolina. In practice, those grants were honored on a preemptive basis, whereby someone who had developed a piece of land in good faith could have it taken away by the presenting of a North Carolina land warrant that predated the current owner's claim. In 1806, Congress created the north-south Congressional Reservation Line, which declared that all land grants issued by North Carolina had to be satisfied east of that line, an area that included about three-fourths of Tennessee. The lands west of the line were not subject to preemption. However, by 1821, the previously reserved western lands were opened to grants. This was necessary because of the continuing presentation of grants, even though many were suspected to be fraudulent.

As Crockett learned the ropes of state government, he also

had to learn where he stood in the opinion of other elected officials. One such lesson came when James C. Mitchell, representing Hamilton, McMinn, and Rhea counties, rose to rebut some position on which Crockett had just spoken. In addressing the chamber, he referred to Crockett as "the gentleman from the cane." Crockett took offense at this phrase as an intentional slight implying that he represented a lesser citizenry and was himself undeserving of respect because he was a backwoodsman. He felt insecure in his knowledge of procedures and was, in fact, probably ill prepared for the job. Nevertheless, he was understandably angered. Crockett insisted on an apology, but none was made. As the body recessed, Crockett confronted Mitchell in the hallway and received in private what he had hoped would be said in the chamber. Mitchell declared that he meant no slight but had only been referring to the geography of Crockett's constituents. Crockett was unsatisfied.

As luck would have it, Crockett that day happened upon, in the street, a cambric ruffle that matched the style of the shirts worn by Mitchell. He promptly pinned it on his coat. When Crockett arose later that day to speak, the awkward contrast of the ruffle

A monument at the courthouse commemorates Murfreesboro as the site of the state capital from 1818 to 1826.

against his backwoods homespun was clear. He paused while the members of the chamber drank in his intention. Boisterous laughter erupted in support of Crockett's display and caused Mitchell to hurriedly retreat from the chamber, embarrassed. Crockett had made a statement about who he was and thereafter used the phrase "gentleman from the cane" as a badge of honor.

Just 12 days into the session, Crockett received a disturbing message that called him back home. He had built a couple of mills and a distillery on Shoal Creek. A flood that arose shortly after he'd left for Murfreesboro had destroyed them all. Crockett stayed at the session to cast his vote for William Carroll as governor, then took leave of the general assembly and rode home to Shoal Creek (see the section on David Crockett State Park, pages 47-50).

After tending to his family, Crockett returned to Murfreesboro for the remainder of the session. He voted in support of matters that would lead to a new state constitution. A revised constitution was necessary, he knew, to increase representation of the people who were pouring into West Tennessee and also to adjust the taxation of land, which was currently favoring the wealthy and established citizens who occupied the better land in Middle Tennessee. Crockett voted to prohibit gaming (a curious position, given his personal fondness for the practice), and he voted against a law that would have allowed the state to hire out debtors for their labor. He had grown up in poverty and believed that his constituents—poor families moving west—would be frequent victims of such a law. In virtually all cases, Crockett voted in support of the westering settlers.

The first session of the 14th General Assembly continued through October and adjourned on November 17, but not before the chambers voted on November 7 to create Carroll County, named for the new governor. Immediately after returning home from the first session, Crockett rode west to the new Carroll County and the Obion River with his son John Wesley. They were preparing to move the family west again (see the section on Rutherford, pages 65-82).

After returning from the Obion River, Crockett learned that a special session of the general assembly had been called for July 22, 1822. The special session met in the First Presbyterian Church on Vine Street in Murfreesboro because the courthouse had burned since the first session. The lower chamber, to which Crockett belonged, met on the ground floor. The upper chamber met in the gallery. During the session, Crockett voted in support of a bill proposing that proceeds from the sale of public lands north and east of the Congressional Reservation Line would go to support education. He also voted against a measure to extend the duration during which land warrants issued by North Carolina could be used east of the line. Again, West Tennessee land issues were important to him. In fact, he was about to become a resident of that area.

In September 1823, Crockett returned to Murfreesboro for the 15th General Assembly as the duly elected representative of the citizens of West Tennessee. He now represented Carroll,

In 1822, the state legislators, including David Crockett, convened at the First Presbyterian Church, which sat on East Vine Street.

Henderson, Humphreys, Madison, and Perry counties. Thanks to his experiences during the previous two sessions, he was now better prepared to legislate. However, he almost immediately created political trouble for himself that would continue into his career.

The term of United States senator John Williams was expiring. Colonel Williams wanted to run for another term. However, he was a longtime opponent of Andrew Jackson and was at odds with those who were grooming Jackson for the presidency in 1824. The Jacksonians wanted Williams out of office. Unfortunately, they could not find a candidate strong enough to defeat Williams without enlisting Jackson himself. At the 11th hour, Jackson agreed to run for the Senate. The vote was conducted by the Tennessee General Assembly, not by popular vote. Jackson won, but Crockett openly voted for Williams, claiming that he had done his job well and deserved to retain his seat. This was Crockett's first break with Jackson, though he proclaimed for years afterward that he still championed the politics that Jackson had originally embraced.

In the 15th General Assembly, Crockett continued to champion the causes of the poor. He voted against using prison labor, since many prisoners were merely debtors. He also voted for improving the navigation of Western rivers and against extending the time frame during which preemptive land warrants could be accepted for lands in West Tennessee. Crockett consistently supported the squatters. He wanted those developing the land to have the first right to buy it. At that stage, Crockett supported the transfer of such land from federal control to the state of Tennessee because he thought Tennessee would treat the squatters favorably. He would later learn he was mistaken.

As the whole country was then in a depression that began with the panic of 1819, Crockett had his suspicions about banks, especially the Second United States Bank, whose practices had brought on the depression. Regarding the pending bills that would regulate state banks, Crockett declared that he thought the banking system was "a species of swindling on a large scale." However, as the current matter before the legislature provided economic relief to poor farmers, he voted in favor of the Bank of Tennessee.

Crockett also proposed prohibiting the retail sale of spirits in connection with elections. Given his reliance on such sales at his campaign appearances, this seems an odd position. However, he did oppose a bill that would have prohibited "tippling houses," or drinking establishments. Crockett also introduced bills to prevent dueling and to encourage marriage with widows. Many find this last issue amusing, given that Crockett's own social and financial status was brought up considerably by his marriage to Elizabeth Patton, whom he recognized only obliquely in the record regarding the bill. (For information about Elizabeth Patton, see the section on Maxwell, pages 41-46.)

The first session of the 15th General Assembly adjourned near the end of November 1823. Crockett went home to the Obion River area. Little is known of his doings before the second session began in September 1824. He did serve as a juror, and court records indicate that many debts he incurred during the period—$9.37, $23.00, $30.00, significant sums in those days—were never repaid.

During the second session of the 15th General Assembly, convened September 20, 1824, by Governor William Carroll, Crockett's district was divided into 10 counties, not five. He thus added Dyer, Fayette, Gibson, Hardeman, and Haywood counties. Crockett voted in favor of taxing land for internal improvements, noting that occupants would pay 12½ cents per 100 acres but that absentee owners would not. He hoped this would encourage the state to put land ownership into the hands of the occupants. Moreover, he continued to protest the actions of speculators who were using unscrupulous practices to force unwitting farmers into losing their land.

After the general assembly adjourned in late October 1824, Crockett returned to his home on the Obion River. Though he had not moved, he no longer lived in Carroll County but in the newly formed Gibson County. During the next year, he was encouraged to run for the United States Congress. Upon doing so, he ended his career in the Tennessee legislature. (For more information, see the section on Rutherford, pages 65-82.)

Lynchburg

A historic marker for the "Crockett Homestead" once stood on TN 55 some 3.5 miles northeast of Lynchburg in Moore County. The marker is missing, but a donated replacement is scheduled to be installed. The marker text read, "One mile south, on the south side of East Branch of Mulberry Creek, David Crockett built a log house in which he lived from 1811-1813. While here he hunted and cleared a field three miles northwest on 'Hungry Hill.' When bears and other game became scarce, he moved to better hunting grounds in Franklin County." Lynchburg is home to the Jack Daniel Distillery, which sits on East Fork Mulberry Creek at TN 55.

After a few years of marriage, two children, and not much success in building a good life for themselves, David and Polly Crockett moved from their rented farm in Jefferson County to new land along the Elk River (see the section on Dandridge, pages 20-28).

The Crocketts loaded up the possessions they could carry on their packhorses. With the help of Polly's father, William Finley, who brought along another horse, they moved "across the mountains," Crockett said, to the Elk River area in Lincoln County. They built a cabin along Mulberry Fork of the Elk River. The unmarked cabin site is today in Moore County just across the Lincoln County line.

The Crocketts lived here "in the years 1809 and '10," Crockett declared. But the dates reported in his autobiography were not always accurate. In this case, Crockett did not leave East Tennessee until September 1811, after the birth of his first two children, John Wesley and William. The Crocketts lived on Mulberry Fork from 1811 until 1813.

Crockett settled a five-acre tract and soon acquired another 15 acres, but he did not intend to concentrate on farming. He found the local hunting good for small game and deer, though bears were scarce, having been hunted extensively.

In 1813, the family moved to Franklin County with the hope of better prospects (see the section on Maxwell, pages 41-46).

Winchester

Winchester is the county seat of Franklin County in south-central Tennessee. It lies at the intersection of US 64 and TN 16 (US 41 Alt.) about 17 miles west of I-24. On the west side of the courthouse square, a marker erected by the Daughters of the American Revolution honors James Winchester, for whom the town was named.

On or about September 9, 1813, David Crockett rode 10 miles from his home, Kentuck, on Rattlesnake Branch of Bean's Creek to

The town was named for James Winchester, Revolutionary War hero and cofounder of Memphis.

Winchester, where men were gathering to join in a campaign against the warring Creeks. The Creeks had massacred nearly the entire contingent of 550 settlers and soldiers at Fort Mims in the Mississippi Territory on the Alabama River.

In the town square at Winchester, local lawyer Francis Jones exhorted the men and whipped them into a patriotic fervor. Crockett was one of the first to step forward, he claimed, in the "large company" that was formed and that came to be known as the Tennessee Volunteer Mounted Riflemen. The men would serve in the regiment of Colonel Newton Cannon for three months. Over the next couple of days, they elected their officers, as was the custom in the militia. Jones—later a United States representative from the area from 1817 to 1821, and the man whose service in Washington preceded that of Congressman Crockett—was made their captain. The men were ordered to reassemble after a week of preparations at their homes.

Franklin County was created in late 1807 from land only recently settled, beginning with those who arrived around 1800. Major William Russell lived on the bluff above Boiling Fork Creek. His home hosted the first court session. In 1809, that site on the bluff was selected as the county seat. It was named to honor General James Winchester, who had served in the Revolutionary War and was the first speaker of the state legislature when Tennessee achieved statehood in 1796. General Winchester's family would play a later role in Crockett's life, as would a member of the Russell family, the latter much sooner than the former.

Until the recent selection of Winchester as the county seat, the business and social center of the county had been Salem on Bean's Creek, not far from Crockett's home (see the next section on Maxwell). Salem sat on a major wagon road through the area. The road led to Huntsville and Baltimore. A road from Salem also went to Nashville. Franklin County was at the time one of the richest cotton-producing areas in the state. Still, in 1813, Winchester was beginning to grow in importance. By the time Crockett arrived, it already had a saloon, probably located south of the courthouse square, where the town's first businesses appeared. Perhaps reflecting relative utility on the frontier, this saloon in Winchester preceded the arrival of a doctor by several years.

Crockett returned to Winchester with provisions and clothing befitting what most thought would be short service. The militia, after reassembling in Winchester, marched some 40 miles toward Huntsville. The men mustered with other militia on September 24 at Beaty's Spring, south of that town (see the section on Huntsville, Alabama, pages 95-99).

Polly Crockett, first wife of David Crockett, was buried near Rattlesnake Branch in Franklin County.

Maxwell

Maxwell, located 9 miles southwest of Winchester in Franklin County, lies along US 64 (David Crockett Highway) at Maxwell Road. Two historic markers on US 64 in Franklin County mentioned a pair of Crockett sites. Neither could be located at the time of this writing, as road construction was prevalent. One in Maxwell read, "Polly Finlay Crockett—David Crockett, his first wife and their children settled on a homestead a few miles east about 1813. She died in 1815, following her husband's return from the Creek War. She is buried in an old cemetery overlooking Bean's Creek, about five miles southeast." The other, located 2.3 miles west of Belvidere, commemorated the site of Crockett's residence along Bean's Creek. It read, "Kentuck—The homestead which David Crockett occupied and named in 1812 is now marked by a well standing in a field 3½ miles south and to the east of this road. From here he went to the Creek War. His first wife died here. In 1816 he married Elizabeth Patton, a widow, and, late in 1817, moved to Lawrence County."

Polly Crockett's grave site is on private property, but respectful visitors are welcomed. From US 64 at Old Bean's Creek Road, a location previously known as Salem and today as Old Salem, go south on Old Bean's Creek Road for one mile to Buncombe Road. Turn left (east) and proceed 3.4 miles to Polly Crockett Lane, a sharp left turn. This gravel road leads a quarter-mile to an unpaved loop near the hilltop. The wooded site is surrounded by fenced pasture. You can walk to the grave, marked by a monolith erected by the Tennessee Historic Commission.

Foster Lane, which connects Maxwell Road and Kentuck Lane, is near Rattlesnake Springs. Driving through this area gives a sense of the landscape where the Crocketts lived.

In 1813, the young Crocketts and their two small children moved from their 20 acres on Mulberry Fork of the Elk River in Lincoln County about 18 miles south-southeast to Franklin County. There, they settled on Rattlesnake Branch of Bean's Creek. Perhaps enamored with the thought of moving to a new frontier, Crockett named his homestead Kentuck—or at least he said he did when writing his autobiography in 1834. Contemplating a run for the presidency, he may have been hoping to persuade the public to think of him as it did celebrated pioneer hero Daniel Boone. In 1813, Boone was 79 years old and living in the Missouri Territory. David Crockett knew him only by reputation; they were two generations apart and separated by a rapidly changing frontier.

On August 30, 1813, a war party of Creeks overran the settlers at Fort Mims in the Mississippi Territory on the Alabama River.

Nearly the entire company of 550 settlers and soldiers was massacred. A few escaped into the forest. (For a more complete account, see the section on Fort Mims, Alabama, pages 121-28.) Reports of the horrors visited upon those at the fort enraged settlers throughout the frontier. Crockett heard about the atrocities, then learned that the militia was mustering 10 miles away at Winchester to retaliate.

Crockett recorded that he was determined to go, but that his wife, Polly, was distraught at his departure. She told him she had no family nearby and no one to help her while he was gone. If he went, she would have the children and a farm to tend all by herself. She pleaded with Crockett not to go. Crockett recorded his thoughts at the time: "My countrymen had been murdered, and I knew that the next thing would be that the Indians would be scalping the women and children all about there, if we didn't put a stop to it. . . . [I] told her that if every man would wait till his wife got willing for him to go to war, there would be no fighting done, until we would all be killed in our own houses." Crockett saw his departure as a duty to his country—or at least the aspiring presidential candidate writing the account in 1834 saw fit to record his feelings in that manner. In any event, Crockett rode off to Winchester and enrolled with the militia (see the preceding section on Winchester, Tennessee, and the section on Ohatchee, Alabama, pages 100-105).

After serving his 90-day enlistment in the fall of 1813, he returned home to his family on Bean's Creek. In his autobiography, Crockett did not offer much information about this period, but no doubt there was much work to be done around the farm. Crockett had never much enjoyed the life of a farmer, and when the call came eight months later to enlist for another tour of duty, he readily took the opportunity despite the fact that Polly was expecting their third child (see the section on Fort Mims, Alabama, pages 121-28).

After completing most of his second tour of duty in the Creek War, Crockett returned home from Fort Strother in the winter of 1814-15. "I found them all well and doing well," Crockett wrote in his autobiography. For the benefit of the national audience to which he addressed his account, he continued with intentional humility, laying claim to his roots as a common man: "Though I was only a rough sort of backwoodsman, they seemed mighty glad to see me, however little the quality folks might suppose it. For I do reckon we love as hard in the backwood country, as any people in the whole creation."

A few weeks later, Crockett was called up again to serve out the remainder of his six-month enlistment. Instead, he gladly allowed an eager young man to go in his place for the balance of his wages. As Crockett had figured, the young man returned after a month or so without having seen any action at all.

Crockett had returned home to a healthy family, and a larger family at that. Polly had given birth to a daughter in early 1815. Whether Crockett was present for the birth or was away in the war is unknown. The daughter was named Margaret, but she was always called Polly, after her mother.

On May 21, 1815, Crockett was elected lieutenant of his militia, having earned respect and notoriety among the people of his county. Unfortunately, the good news ended there, as tragedy soon struck the family. During the summer, Crockett's wife died. He gave few details in his autobiography about the circumstances. Perhaps that was because others later in his life hinted that he was in some way at fault for leaving her alone while he went away to fight in the Creek War. Nor did he attribute her death to complications from the birth of their third child. He said only that "in this time, I met with the hardest trial which ever falls to the lot of man. Death, that cruel leveler of all distinctions—to whom the prayers and tears of husbands, and of even helpless infancy, are addressed in vain—entered my humble cottage, and tore from my children an affectionate good mother, and from me a tender and loving wife."

Crockett was immediately faced with the challenge of raising his family—including an infant daughter—alone. He called upon his youngest brother and the brother's family to come live at Bean's Creek. For reasons Crockett did not mention, the arrangement did not work out. What he needed was another wife.

A young woman in the Bean's Creek community had lost her husband during the Creek War. She had two small children about the age of Crockett's. He wrote that she owned "a snug little farm," and he knew her to be an "industrious" woman. Crockett began to pursue a relationship with Elizabeth Patton, knowing that a woman on the frontier with her means and abilities would be pursued by others as well. It was known that in addition to the farm, she possessed $800 in cash, a considerable sum.

Though the courtship may have had some passion to it, Crockett's description made it sound businesslike and his courting almost devious: "I began to think, that as we were both in the same situation, it might be that we could do something for each other. . . . I soon began to pay my respects to her in real good earnest; but I was as sly about it as a fox when he is going to rob a hen-roost."

Twenty-one months younger than Crockett, Elizabeth Patton was a sensible, practical woman who saw the same opportunity. "We soon bargained, and got married," Crockett wrote. She became the stepmother to his three children and he the stepfather to her two. Later, they had children together.

The wedding was held in the home of Elizabeth Patton in the spring or summer of 1816, most likely within a year of Polly Crockett's untimely passing. Friends and family gathered for the occasion. A minister, rather than a justice of the peace, most likely performed the ceremony. While the assembled guests were waiting for the bride to enter the room, a grunting pig wandered through the doorway. The solemnity of the occasion broken, the children began to laugh. At that point, Crockett walked over and shooed the pig out the door, remarking in words perhaps better suited to a bachelor party than a wedding party, "Old hook, from now on, I'll do the grunting around here."

A few months after the wedding, Crockett rode into the Black Warrior Valley to look at land he had previously seen that might offer opportunity for settling. He was already thinking of moving west (see the section on Tuscaloosa, Alabama, pages 115-21).

After Crockett returned from exploring the Black Warrior Valley in 1816, he spent some time recovering from an illness he had contracted there, most likely malaria. During his recuperation, he decided to make another trip due west to look at land east of the Tennessee River as it flowed north, land that had been made available by Andrew Jackson's treaty with the Chickasaws in September 1816. In the fall of 1817, probably after he had completed the harvest, Crockett rode west to explore Shoal Creek (see the next section on David Crockett State Park).

David Crockett State Park includes the land on which Crockett built a powder mill, gristmill, and distillery.

David Crockett State Park

Sitting one mile west of Lawrenceburg on US 64 in Lawrence County in south-central Tennessee, David Crockett State Park includes the headwaters of Shoal Creek. The park commemorates Crockett's building a gristmill, powder mill, and distillery at this site around 1821. A visitor center interprets his life in the area. A fire in the late 1960s destroyed much of the memorabilia and artifacts previously collected.

A historic marker along US 64 at Shoal Creek near the entrance to the park was missing at the time of this writing. It read, "Crockett's Mill—About two miles north, on Shoal Creek, David Crockett built a grist mill, powder mill, and distillery about 1819. In 1821, flood water from the creek destroyed his installation and bankrupted him. Shortly thereafter, he moved to the vicinity of Rutherford, in west Tennessee, leaving his remaining property to creditors."

In 1817, David Crockett was again looking for an opportunity to make his fortune on the westward-moving frontier. Following his first few years of marriage, he had moved over the mountains to land along Mulberry Fork and later Bean's Creek. He had served in the Creek War and suffered the death of his wife, Polly. Remarried, Crockett wanted to establish a new life for his second, combined family. He revisited the Black Warrior River area he had seen during the war but found it lacking. In fact, he almost died on that trip, and his untimely passing was reported prematurely to his family (see the section on Tuscaloosa, Alabama, pages 118-21). In light of that experience, Crockett chose to look west, rather than south, from his home at Bean's Creek.

Probably after he helped with the harvest, Crockett rode west to explore the lands recently opened for settlement through a September 1816 treaty concluded between Andrew Jackson and the Chickasaws. The treaty opened new lands east of the Tennessee River as it flowed north to the Ohio River. On his trip west, Crockett suffered a relapse of his malaria and fell ill with what he called "ague and fever," which he blamed on sleeping outside on the damp ground. In his weakened condition, he traveled no farther than 80 miles from his home. Still, he found the headwaters of Shoal Creek an inviting place and decided to move his family there.

Perhaps as early as September 1817, the family packed its belongings and moved west. By December, the Crocketts had leased part of their Franklin County farm and received a cash payment for its use. During the interim months, they established themselves in their new home.

At the time they moved to Shoal Creek, it was beyond Giles County, the westernmost county with any established government. For a while, legal business was conducted in Giles County. Lawrence

In 1821, Shoal Creek flooded and destroyed Crockett's recently completed mills and distillery.

County was formed on October 21, 1817. On November 25, Crockett was made a justice of the peace. Later, he became a court referee (see the next section on Lawrenceburg).

Sometime in 1821, Crockett borrowed money and built a business enterprise along Shoal Creek, erecting facilities that cost about $3,000. His wife, Elizabeth, managed the enterprise profitably. However, in September 1821, while Crockett was serving his first term in the Tennessee General Assembly (see the section on Murfreesboro, pages 29-37), a flood on Shoal Creek destroyed everything: his powder mill, his gristmill, and his distillery. Crockett left Murfreesboro and rode home immediately. "The first news that I heard after I got to the Legislature, was, that my mills were . . . swept away all to smash by a large fresh, that came soon after I left home," he wrote. "The misfortune just made a complete mash of me." Reflecting on the incident a dozen years latter, he chose to praise Elizabeth: "Best of all, I had an honest wife. She didn't advise me as is too fashionable, to smuggle up this, and that, and t'other to go on at home; but she told me, says she, 'Just pay up, as long as you have a bit's worth in the world; and then every-body will be satisfied, and we will scuffle for more.' This was just such talk as I wanted to hear, for a man's wife can hold him devil-ish uneasy, if she begins to scold and fret, and perplex him, at a time when he has a full load for a railroad car on his mind already."

During this leave of absence, Crockett probably concluded that his land would be lost to pay off the debts he had incurred to build the mills and distillery. Accordingly, he moved his family to lodg-ing probably provided by local family members. Both the Pattons and the Crocketts had moved west to join David and Elizabeth in Lawrence County. Settlement in the area was growing. Indeed, others already occupied his Shoal Creek property just one month after the flood.

After the session of the Tennessee General Assembly ended in November 1821, Crockett rode west from Lawrence County to the Obion River area to prepare a home for his family (see the section on Rutherford, pages 65-82). When he returned to Lawrenceburg after late April 1822 from his land on Rutherford Fork of the Obion River, he was notified that Governor William Carroll had called a special session of the general assembly to con-vene July 22. To fulfill his civic responsibilities, he rode off to Murfreesboro again.

A statue of David Crockett, fashioned after the 1834 John Gadsby Chapman painting, was erected in 1922.

Lawrenceburg

Lawrenceburg, the county seat of Lawrence County, sits at the intersection of US 64 and US 43 in south-central Tennessee. Military Street is 0.2 mile west of US 43. It leads south from US 64 (Gaines Avenue) for one block to a David Crockett statue and monument. Farther south on Military Street, a historic marker honoring Crockett is located a half-block south of East Taylor Street. The marker sits in front of the David Crockett Museum at 218 South Military Street.

It was in Lawrence County that David Crockett became civically and politically active. He was a leading citizen of the frontier community. He served as a justice of the peace and as a town commissioner. After learning how to campaign on the frontier, he represented the county in the Tennessee General Assembly. Between sessions of the assembly in Murfreesboro in 1821 and 1822, he rode northwest and established a new home in West Tennessee, then returned to move his family.

In 1818, Crockett served as a justice of the peace in Lawrence County. In describing his years as an administrator of justice, he took some pains in his 1834 autobiography to remind readers that he was but a common man who shared in spirit with others on the frontier. "At first, whenever I told my constable, says I—'Catch that fellow and bring him up for trial,'—away he went, and the fellow must come, dead or alive," he wrote. Crockett explained that the spoken word was good enough for him, but that the legislature required him to write his warrants. "This was a hard business on me, for I could barely write my own name; but to do this and write the warrants too, was at least a huckleberry over my persimmons." He continued, "I gave my decisions on the principles of common justice and honesty between man and man, and relied on natural born sense, and not on law learning to guide me; for I had never read a page in a law book in all my life." It is interesting to note that a law book presented by Crockett to a friend in 1828 is on display at the Alamo in San Antonio, Texas.

Crockett's likability worked in his favor. While living in Lawrence County, he was approached by a Captain Matthews, who intended to run for colonel of the militia, an elected position. The captain asked Crockett if he would run for first major and thus support Matthews's bid for colonel. Finally persuaded to seek that position, Crockett later attended a corn husking and frolic hosted by Captain Matthews. There, it was revealed that the captain's own son was running against Crockett for major. When Crockett confronted the elder Matthews on the matter, the captain said he hated that his son had to run against someone as popular as Crockett. Crockett then advised him that he should not fret about his son's predicament at all because Crockett now intended to run against the captain for the colonelcy. Taking the confrontation in stride, Captain Matthews called the large crowd to gather around and introduced Crockett as his new opponent, perhaps thinking Crockett was not accustomed to speaking in public. The captain spoke first and Crockett followed, sharing how he had decided to run. "I told the people the cause of my opposing him," Crockett later wrote, "remarking that as I had the whole family to run against any way, I was determined to levy on the head of the mess." When the votes were cast, Crockett was elected lieutenant colonel-commandant and another man was elected major. Both the Matthewses were defeated soundly.

In early 1818, the local citizens again showed the esteem in which they held Crockett by making him a town commissioner in Lawrenceburg. Serving simultaneously as commissioner and justice of the peace, he dealt with the typical issues of a growing community, including land disputes, road building, property taxes, and voter rolls.

Crockett resigned his court responsibilities in November 1819; some 14 months later, he also resigned as a town commissioner. Free to seek higher office, he undertook that challenge with vigor. In February 1821, he offered his name for a seat in the Tennessee legislature representing Lawrence and Hickman counties. He was subsequently elected. To serve his new office, he rode to Murfreesboro, where the 14th General Assembly convened on September 17, 1821 (see the section on Murfreesboro, pages 29-37).

After the session was completed late that fall, Crockett rode off to his land in Carroll County to establish a new home. Upon his return to Lawrence County in the spring of 1822 from his trip to the Obion River country, he found that several lawsuits had been filed against him, principally arising from the loss of his mills. Crockett gave his power of attorney to Mansil Crisp to settle all his debts as best he could. It is believed that Crockett's landholdings in Lawrence County were sufficient for that purpose. Crockett then prepared to attend the second session of the 14th General Assembly, which Governor William Carroll had called to convene on July 22. When that session ended in August, Crockett loaded up his family and moved west to the Obion River country (see the section on Rutherford, pages 65-82).

Centerville

Centerville, about 55 miles southwest of Nashville, has been the county seat of Hickman County since 1823. The town square is at the intersection of TN 48/TN 100 and Old Highway 50. This square was the site of an early Crockett speech in his campaign for a seat in the Tennessee legislature.

Vernon is six miles north-northwest of Centerville. A historic marker on TN 230 at Old Airport Road, 2.0 miles west of TN 48, commemorates the first courthouse there.

In February 1821, David Crockett put his name forward for a seat in the Tennessee General Assembly, then left home with a drove of horses headed for North Carolina, probably to his father-in-law's home in Swannanoa. After a three-month absence, he returned and began his campaign in June for the August election. He arrived in Hickman County just in time for a frolic, to be preceded by a two-day squirrel hunt along the Duck River. It was a contest according to which the team returning with the fewest squirrel scalps had to pay for the cost of the party. Crockett was probably considered a ringer. Indeed, his marksmanship helped his team to win. "The company had every thing to eat and drink that could be furnished in so new a country," wrote Crockett, "and much fun and good humor prevailed."

Eventually, Crockett was called upon to speak to those assembled. He addressed the crowd uncertain of what he would say and how he would get the words out. "I made many apologies and tried to get off, for I know'd I had a man to run against who could speak prime, and I know'd, too, that I wasn't able to shuffle and cut with him," he later wrote. But Crockett managed to please the audience with the homespun humor he was just developing as his trademark. "I got up and told the people I reckoned they know'd what I had come for, but if not, I could tell them. I had come for their votes, and if they didn't watch mighty close, I'd get them too."

Continuing in this, his first political speech, Crockett soon found he'd lost his way. He then told the crowd he supposed he was like the man who slapped his hand against an empty barrel declaring that he'd had some cider from that barrel a few days before and was now trying to see if any was still there. If there was, the fellow lamented, he couldn't get it out. "I told them," wrote Crockett, "that there had been a little bit of a speech in me a while ago, but I believed I couldn't get it out." When they roared with laughter, he knew he had won over the audience. He continued with a few more anecdotes and then, declaring he was thirsty, suggested that a drink was just what they all needed. Crockett left the stage and headed to the stand that sold libations, most of the audience following him there. While they drank, he regaled them with more stories. He stayed there for the time it took his opponents to complete their speeches, which were delivered to a much-diminished audience across the way.

Following that success, Crockett moved on to nearby Vernon for a Saturday feast prior to Monday's court. Vernon was then the county seat, and Crockett could not be pinned down on his position as to whether or not the seat should be moved to Centerville. A large crowd gathered to hear speeches from a host of candidates, including those running for Congress and governor. These were all accomplished orators who were well practiced at speaking for long periods. Fortunately, Crockett's turn came late in the series of speakers. After listening to politicians all day, the audience was exhausted. Crockett recognized this. He rose from his seat and told a tale that he referred to in his autobiography as "some laughable story." In that manner, he secured the favor of the people. He learned an important lesson that politicians have recognized ever since: People don't want to be informed, they want to be entertained.

Assured that he was well liked, Crockett did not return to Hickman County until after the election, which he won handily, more than doubling his opponent's number of votes (see the section on Lawrenceburg, pages 51-54).

Jackson

Jackson is located in Madison County in West Tennessee along I-40 between Memphis and Nashville. A plaque on the Madison County Courthouse lawn commemorates David Crockett and his famous "I will go to Texas" farewell, addressed to all the citizens who voted for his opponent, Adam Hunts-

man of Madison County. Most historians contend that Crockett made the declaration first in Memphis. Also, the marker dates the event incorrectly as 1831 instead of 1835.

The grave of Adam Huntsman, who defeated Crockett in 1835 for his seat in Congress, is located east of Jackson in Old Salem Cemetery. From US 70 at Flex Drive, proceed one mile east to Cotton Grove Road, then go north for 0.3 mile to Old Salem Cemetery.

As expected, the 1833 campaign for a congressional seat from Tennessee was hard-fought. The Jacksonians poured resources into the fight, as did David Crockett's supporters and the Eastern alliance that was championing him. The politics of the time revolved around removal of the Indians, tariffs and nullification, and banking. New Englanders disapproved of removing the Indians, and Southerners opposed a tariff, which they threatened to nullify if passed. These forces joined with the Second United States Bank to oppose

A plaque at the Madison County Courthouse commemorates Crockett's infamous departing words—in 1835, not 1831—to his West Tennessee constituents.

The grave of Adam Huntsman, who defeated Crockett in 1835, is in Old Salem Cemetery.

Andrew Jackson, who believed the bank was a monopoly. The Jackson opponents seized on Crockett as a likely candidate to further their efforts to discredit Jackson. Crockett was popular with Western voters and was opposed to Jackson, though for reasons not necessarily related to the interests of his supporters. Crockett's staunch opposition to Jackson may well have blinded him to how he was being used politically by the anti-Jackson forces.

Two factors worked against Crockett's election in 1833.

First, the Jacksonians had been able to gerrymander the counties so that Crockett's support was divided between the new 12th and 13th districts, both carved from the Ninth, in which Crockett had previously run. For example, Crockett's new district included Madison County, which was against him, but took away Shelby County, which was decidedly in his corner. The arrangement appeared so illogical to residents of the newly formed districts that they felt it was done only for political purposes. In his autobiography, Crockett declared of the new districts, "They are certainly the most unreasonably laid off of any in the state, or perhaps in the nation, or even in the te-total creation."

The other major factor working against Crockett was the creative political writings of Adam Huntsman, an attorney in the town of Jackson and an ardent supporter of Andrew Jackson. Writing under the pen name "Black Hawk," Huntsman published his "Chronicles" in the newspapers. Taking a biblical tone, he parodied national politics and Crockett's role in them. Huntsman wrote, "And it came to pass in those days when Andrew was chief Ruler over the Children of Columbia, that there arose a mighty man in the river country, whose name was David." He wrote in support of William Fitzgerald, the incumbent congressman from the Ninth District who was Crockett's opponent in 1833.

Crockett campaigned in earnest, taking pride in the fact that he was not beholden to President Jackson. "Look at my arms, you will find no party hand-cuff on them," he wrote in his autobiography. "Look at my neck, you will not find there any collar, with the engraving 'MY DOG, Andrew Jackson.' " In addition, the residents of the 12th District did not appreciate the gerrymandering of their area. Crockett wrote that when it came time to vote, the residents showed "that they were not to be transferred like hogs . . . in the market." He won by a narrow margin of 202 votes and returned to Congress in 1833 for a third term.

Crockett's congressional victory was encouraging to the Whigs. After Jackson was reelected president in 1832, the Whigs began their search for a national candidate they could support. One faction favored David Crockett and asked him to run for president. Although the Whig leaders may have genuinely thought Crockett a viable national candidate, they may also have been planning to run a wide field of candidates in which no one would be a clear winner. That would throw the 1836 presidential election into the House of Representatives, where the Whigs believed they could prevail, as John Quincy Adams had done over Jackson in 1824. In either case, Crockett was asked through the Mississippi State Convention in December 1833 to offer himself as a presidential candidate. This invitation came as he was working on his autobiography. He must have been quite taken with the notion, as he made several references in his writings to the prospect of serving as president. In a clear reference to Andrew Jackson's war record and his path to the White House, Crockett wrote, "I must give an account of the part I took in the defence of the country. If it should make me President, why I can't help it." (For information on Crockett's tenure in the nation's capital, see the section on Washington, District of Columbia, pages 157-69).

In the spring of 1835, Crockett left Washington for his home in Tennessee. He had only a few months to campaign among his constituents to retain his seat in Congress. Once again, he was returning to them without having gotten the Tennessee Vacant Land Bill passed by Congress. Still, he was popular in West Tennessee and elsewhere. He was indeed a national figure.

Throughout the campaign of 1835, Crockett was helped by the publication of letters in an anti-Jackson weekly called the *Downing Gazette*. Major Jack Downing was a fictitious character created by publisher Seba Smith, who wrote from Portland, Maine. During Crockett's tour of Eastern cities in 1834, he had met in New York with "the rale [real] Major Jack Downing," Crockett wrote. It appears that he agreed to have Smith pen a few letters ostensibly from Crockett to appear in the *Downing Gazette*. From March until August 1835, Smith, previously a strong Jackson supporter, wrote several anti-Jackson letters that appeared to be from Crockett, some reportedly from his home in "Weekly" (Weakley) County. They included enough personal information to make them credible to readers, though scholars can clearly distinguish them from Crockett originals.

Even given his national prominence, Crockett still had to pay attention to his constituents at home, as they were the voters who would return him to Congress. He campaigned vigorously. His opponent was Adam Huntsman, a well-known figure in Madison County. Huntsman had previously opposed Crockett's candidacy through his "Chronicles." Now, he was opposing him as a candidate.

Having lost a leg in the Creek War, Huntsman walked on a wooden peg. Popular among men, he was also known to be a bit of a womanizer. Those credentials play into a story told about the Crockett-Huntsman campaign. Many historians accept it as fact.

During the campaign of 1835, Crockett and Huntsman were traveling together. On one particular night, they stopped to enjoy the hospitality of a well-to-do farmer, who put both men in the same room. Down the outside porch was the room where the farmer's young, unmarried daughter retired. As the tale was told, after Huntsman fell asleep, Crockett crept down the porch, taking a wooden ladder-back chair with him. He rattled the door of the young woman's room. Then, as she screamed, he hobbled back to his room, one foot placed in the chair so as to make it sound like a wooden leg on the porch. Crockett jumped back into bed just before the farmer broke into their room and railed against Huntsman, who was then just awakening from sleep. The farmer declared that he had heard Huntsman's peg leg tapping along the porch, and he certainly knew of his reputation with women. Playing the peacemaker, Crockett secured the farmer's pledge that he would vote for him and would also encourage all that he knew to do the same in the face of Huntsman's apparent impropriety.

Regardless of Crockett's antics, when August 6 came and the votes were tallied, he had lost. Adam Huntsman beat him by 230 votes to become the new United States congressman for the district. Crockett would find another adventure. It involved a search for new land and new wealth. It also fulfilled his promise to leave the country. David Crockett was heading to Texas.

After three months of preparation for his departure (see the section on Rutherford, pages 65-82), Crockett's party of four riders left his home in Gibson County on November 1 and arrived in Jackson. It was probably here that they learned about the fight at Gonzales and the revolution in Texas. Crockett may well have changed his mind in Jackson about what he wanted to do in Texas. In addition to looking at land to improve his fortune, he probably decided that a good fight was brewing, through which he could possibly improve his political future. (For more information, see the section on Memphis, pages 87-94.)

Trenton

Trenton, the county seat of Gibson County, is located in west-central Tennessee at the convergence of TN 367, TN 186, and TN 77. US 45W bypasses the town to its east. The courthouse is located on the town square at the intersection of College Street (TN 367) and Eaton Street (TN 104). A bust of David Crockett occupies the southeast corner of the courthouse square. Gibson County was formed in 1824 by legislation initiated by Crockett while he was a Tennessee legislator. The striking courthouse, erected in 1899, is the fourth on this site.

In 1827, Crockett began in earnest his run for the United States Congress. He had run in 1825, but only reluctantly, and he had been defeated. For this second campaign, he had better prospects because of the financial support he received from Marcus B. Winchester of Memphis and because his opponent, the incumbent, Colo-

At the courthouse in Trenton, David Crockett
is celebrated as a famous resident of
Gibson County.

nel Adam Alexander, had voted for a high tariff on cotton. In 1825,
cotton sold for $25 for 100 pounds, and the tariff had not been a
deciding issue. By 1827, the price had fallen, and Alexander's earlier position was an unpopular one. But perhaps the best advantage
Crockett had was that he was an entertaining candidate. As he
wrote in his autobiography, "I was able to buy a little of 'the creature,' to put my friends in a good humour as well as the other
gentlemen for they all treat in that country."

Crockett had three opponents. Early in the contest, he bewil-
dered one of them badly. It seems that Crockett had been telling
exaggerations and total falsehoods about this fellow, who was outraged. The man contrived to show up Crockett by having present
at one of their joint presentations witnesses who could prove that
Crockett was slandering him. Crockett must have got wind of this
plot. He gave his usual delivery, in which he told much about the
opponent that was false, then prepared to leave the stage. Almost
as an afterthought, Crockett stopped and turned to the crowd.

Declaring that his opponent had planned to trap him in his lies, Crockett readily admitted that what he'd said about the man was untrue. He felt entitled to do so, he continued, because all the candidates lied about each other. The crowd roared its approval. Any attempt the other candidate could then have made to call Crockett a liar would only have improved Crockett's standing. The candidate withdrew from the race, declaring that he could not serve such an irrational population that would prefer a liar to represent them.

On another day, Crockett had occasion to show up one of the other candidates as well. The remaining two rival candidates fancied themselves the only viable options. Even though Crockett had spoken first that day, the third candidate never addressed his remarks to anything Crockett had said. It so happened that while the man was speaking, a flock of guineas appeared and created such a racket that the candidate asked that they be shooed away. When the candidate finished his remarks, Crockett rose and addressed the audience, declaring that this fellow was the only man he had ever

A marker commemorating David Crockett was erected by the Daughters of the American Revolution at the Gibson County Public Library.

seen besides himself who could understand birds. When asked what he meant, Crockett explained that the man had been so ill-mannered in not addressing Crockett's remarks that when the guineas called out, "Crockett, Crockett, Crockett," the man had called for them to be silenced. The crowd roared its approval of this clever turn, at which the candidate was quite miffed.

When the votes were tallied, Crockett had won the election. Before he went to Washington, he traveled with his son John Wesley and his wife, Elizabeth, to her family's plantation in Swannanoa, North Carolina. Along the way, Crockett became ill with what he called "biles [bilious] fever." It delayed his arrival a few weeks, but he and his family did reach Swannanoa in time for one of the most infamous events of the era (see the section on Tuxedo, North Carolina, pages 142-48). From there, Crockett rode in a carriage to Washington by way of East Tennessee, while his family returned to Rutherford. Four weeks later, Crockett was in the nation's capital as a duly elected member of the United States Congress (see the section on Washington, District of Columbia, pages 157-69).

Rutherford

Rutherford is located in Gibson County in West Tennessee at US 45W Business (Trenton Street) and TN 105. The new alignment of US 45W bypasses Rutherford. The town's water tower proudly proclaims Rutherford to be "The Last Home of Davy Crockett." A commemorative site on Trenton Street is called "The Last Home of Davy Crockett and Grave of His Mother." It includes a replica cabin filled with Crockett memorabilia and artifacts of the frontier life. The remains of Rebecca Hawkins Crockett were reinterred at the town-owned site. The

Davy Crockett Museum is run by volunteers. The staff there can direct visitors to other Crockett sites in the area. Not all of them, such as the grave site of Robert Patton, David's father-in-law, are marked on the ground.

The "First Cabin Site of Davy Crockett" is commemorated by a hand-carved sign on Somers Road 0.2 mile west of TN 445. Somers Road is 1.6 miles north along TN 445 from TN 105 about a mile east of town.

David Crockett moved to Rutherford Fork of the Obion River in West Tennessee to make his family's new home. His bear-hunting exploits there earned him notoriety. Using his newfound celebrity status, he became more engaged in state politics and eventually entered the national political scene. From his home on Rutherford Fork, Crockett campaigned in 1823 for reelection to the Tennessee General Assembly. In 1825, he sought a seat in Congress but lost. During all his campaigning and subsequent tenure as an elected public servant, Crockett traveled from his home to communities in his district, to Murfreesboro, and eventually to Washington, returning when the assemblies were not in session and when the campaigning was done. He won a seat in Congress in 1827 and 1829 but lost the election in 1831. He re-

Crockett's first cabin, built in 1821 on Rutherford Fork, was a quarter-mile south of this marker.

gained his seat in 1833 but lost it again in 1835. That fall, he left his home in Rutherford to explore Texas.

In the late fall of 1821, after his first session in the Tennessee General Assembly adjourned in November, Crockett prepared for his family's move west. He, his oldest son, John Wesley, age 14, and a young man named Abram Henry rode from Lawrence County to the Obion River region to examine land Crockett had purchased from his father-in-law, Robert Patton. Patton had acquired the property through a land warrant he had received for his service during the American Revolution (see the section on Swannanoa, North Carolina, pages 136-40).

Crockett and his son selected a cabin site and then with Henry set out almost due north for seven miles to see the Owens family, the nearest neighbors. They lived across the Obion River, and the travel was not easy. The land the small party crossed had been terribly tortured by the New Madrid earthquake of December 1811 and the 2,000 aftershocks that had followed for more than a year (see the next section on Reelfoot Lake State Park). On top of that, high winds had felled trees and created a snarl of brush and timber that hindered passage. Crockett called these snarls "harracanes." Fortunately, the conditions had also created a forest in which game of every kind had multiplied unmolested for years. The region was as rich with deer and fowl as the lands farther east had been a generation earlier. It was a hunter's paradise, and Crockett was one of the first to arrive.

The Obion River was out of its banks. Because the region was so flat, the land was flooded for miles along the river's course. Despite the extreme cold of December, Crockett's party waded into the water a half-mile before reaching the river itself. The men were on foot and had one packhorse for their provisions. Sometimes, they were neck-deep in water, walking slowly as Crockett used a pole to assure his footing ahead of the others. He recalled in his autobiography how pitiful his young son looked, shivering in the brutal cold as they made their way toward the river. When they arrived, Crockett used his hatchet to chop down a tree. He felled it toward another blown down toward them from the other side. A footbridge was formed where the two crowns met, allowing the party to make its way across the river. There, they resumed their wading without yet being able to see land ahead. They walked and waded for a mile before emerging onto higher ground wet, cold, and exhausted.

When Crockett's three-person troupe appeared at the Owens house, the residents were astonished to see them. Some boatmen making their way up the Obion River had stopped at the Owens home and were equally startled to see the three hunters emerge from the flood plain. They all retreated into the home, where Mrs. Owens tended to John Wesley. The family's hospitality was gracious. Mr. Owens put out his bottle, and all three, including John Wesley, "took a strong pull at it," Crockett wrote. "I concluded that if a horn wasn't good then, there was no use for its invention." Soon, the men had warmed themselves inside and out before the fire.

That night, all the men—excluding John Wesley, who stayed at the cabin with Mrs. Owens—went aboard the boat and drank rather heavily from the liquor on board. The boat was set to make its way to McLemore's Bluff, yet another 30 miles inland, to demonstrate that boats could in fact reach that point. For completing this promotional stunt, the boatmen would receive $500 plus the profits they would get from selling the cargo they carried: flour, coffee, salt, sugar, whiskey, and other trade goods.

Seeing an opportunity, Crockett enticed the boatmen to return with him to his new homesite and help him erect a cabin. They

The last home of David Crockett is interpreted by a replica cabin and museum in Rutherford.

brought along some goods for which Crockett would trade: four barrels of meal, one barrel of salt, and 10 gallons of whiskey. "We slapped up a cabin in little or no time," Crockett wrote.

To pay for his purchases and for the boatmen's help with the cabin, Crockett agreed to help them on their course upriver. Preparing to leave, he killed a deer and took a side of bacon from the provisions he had received from the boatmen. He left these vittles with Abram Henry and John Wesley, who stayed at the cabin while Crockett proceeded upriver with the boatmen.

When they reached what looked to be an impassable snarl of timber, Crockett left the boatmen to hunt for deer. He began to follow a herd of elk whose tracks he had seen. Throughout the day as he pursued the elk, he continued to come across deer. He dropped six in all and hung each one up with plans to retrieve them later. He then returned to the spot where he had left the boatmen. To his surprise, they were gone. He hollered for a while without success, then fired off a shot, to which the boatmen responded. They were two miles away and very near where Crockett had dropped his last deer. He set off following the river. "It was now dark," he wrote, "and I had to crawl through the fallen timber the best way

I could . . . for the vines and briers had grown all through it, and so thick that a good fat coon couldn't much more than get along." He fired another shot as he approached the water. The boatmen then used their skiff to retrieve him from the bank. He was exhausted and glad to be aboard. A horn or two and a good meal revived him, though he later wrote of being "so tired that I could hardly work my jaws to eat."

In the morning, Crockett and one of the boatmen headed into the woods and retrieved four of the deer. They left the other two still hanging. They then embarked with the crew on their continued trip upstream.

The journey to McLemore's Bluff took 11 days, rather than the six or seven Crockett had told his son he would be away. In appreciation for his help, the boatmen gave him the skiff. Shortly afterward, Crockett set off downriver for his cabin. He was joined by Flavius Harris, who intended to live with the Crocketts.

All hands went to work in the spring. Crockett's party cleared a field and put in a crop. Crockett wrote, "I made corn enough to do me, and during that spring I killed ten bears, and a great abundance of deer." He saw no other settlers during that time except the Owenses and some passengers on the river. "Indians, though, were still plenty enough," he wrote.

In the late spring, Crockett returned the 150 miles to Lawrence County to retrieve his family. But first he had to attend a special session of the general assembly called by Governor William Carroll (see the section on Murfreesboro, pages 29-37).

After attending the second session of the 14th General Assembly in Murfreesboro, which adjourned around August 24, Crockett returned 80 miles to Lawrence County, packed his family, and then rode 150 miles to their new Carroll County home. The move was completed by early September 1822.

During the next year, Crockett immersed himself in building a new life. The scant records show that he served on juries and submitted wolf scalps to the court for the three-dollar bounty paid. But trouble apparently followed him, too. He was indicted for assault and sued for debt.

In his own account, Crockett told more heroic tales. In the fall of 1822, after he had harvested his first crop of corn, he went hunting to provision his family for the winter. He was quite successful but found that he was nearly out of powder. He lamented that he would not even have powder for firing his guns to celebrate Christmas, as was the custom. Fortunately, Crockett had a brother-in-law who had moved west also and lived only six miles away, across the Obion River from Rutherford Fork. Crockett had asked the fellow to bring him a barrel of powder but had never retrieved it. Despite Elizabeth's considerable protests, Crockett set out in the frigid cold and snow to get it. He wrote of his wife, "She said, we had as well starve for me to freeze to death or to get drowned, and one or the other was certain if I attempted to go."

Crockett headed out the door into four inches of snow. He had considerable clothing wrapped around him and an extra change as well, should he get wet, which was inevitable. Within a quarter-mile, he began to wade in the water covering the flood plain a mile from the swollen main channel. He crossed the channel without incident and was making his way across a wide, deep slough. From previous ventures, he knew there was a log he could cross. Failing to see it, he concluded it was submerged. He felled a small tree toward where he thought the log should be and waded into the water with a pole, feeling his way along the submerged log. It was three feet below the water's surface. Crockett shuffled along the log, taking small steps. "It was a mighty ticklish business," he wrote. By the time he crossed, his feet and legs were numb, but he still had a distance to go. Upon reaching another log he had to cross, he discovered this one was floating. Undeterred, he started across, but the log rolled when he was in the middle, and he fell in the icy water. Fortunately, he was able to hold his bundle of dry clothes out of the water with his rifle. He made his way out of the water and changed clothes, shivering. Determined to warm himself, he tried to trot along the trail. Forcing himself along, he continued five miles to the home of his brother-in-law, where the family was greatly surprised to see him out in such weather.

Indeed, the weather had turned bitterly cold. Crockett was persuaded to delay his return trip. During the next two days, he hunted, killing two deer and stalking a bear that had not yet gone into hibernation. On the third day, he took the keg of powder and headed for home, recognizing that his family had no meat.

The water was now frozen. Crockett attempted to walk on the ice, but it was not strong enough to support him with the added weight of the powder. He broke through and had to wade in the frigid water, using his tomahawk to break the ice before him. The log that had thrown him was frozen into place; he crossed it without mishap. In other places, Crockett was forced to wade. "By this time I was nearly frozen to death," he wrote. After crossing the main channel, he saw what he thought he recognized as bear tracks in the snow. He primed his rifle and followed them, determined to catch a prize. But the suspicious tracks led him home and indeed to his front door. Elizabeth, worried about David, had sent one of the young men who worked on the farm to look for him— or for evidence that he had died. "When I got home," Crockett wrote, "I wasn't quite dead, but mighty nigh it; but had my powder, and that was what I went for."

In a few days, David's brother-in-law came to the Crockett cabin so they could hunt together. The brother-in-law was hunting for turkey, but Crockett was determined to shoot a bear. "I told them I had dreamed the night before," he wrote, "of having . . . a battle with a bear; for in bear country, I never know'd such a dream to fail." After the men had bagged a few turkeys, Crockett's hunting dogs began to act strange. He followed them as they pursued a scent and found them barking at the base of an empty tree. Crockett was put out with his dogs. "I was so infernal mad," he wrote, "that I determined if I could get near enough, to shoot the old hound dog at least." He pushed on with his dogs and came to an open prairie where he saw a large black bear weighing perhaps 600 pounds. "He looked, at the distance he was from me, like a large black bull," Crockett wrote. He knew then that his dogs had been waiting for him to catch up with them. "I took my gobblers from my back and hung them up in a sapling, and broke like a quarter horse after my bear, for the sight of him had put new springs in me." Crockett climbed through snarls and thickets until he got within 80 yards of the bear. He fired into the animal's chest as it rose, then quickly

The Crockett museum has rooms with an assortment of memorabilia and antiques.

loaded and fired again as close as he could to the same spot. The bear fell and grabbed one of the dogs. Crockett ran to the wounded animal wielding his tomahawk and knife, upon which the bear released the dog and looked straight at him. "I got back in all sorts of a hurry, for I know'd if he got hold of me, he would hug me altogether too close for comfort." Crockett retreated to get his rifle and fired a third and fatal shot. Faced with the task of getting the meat home, he blazed a trail back to the cabin and returned with his brother-in-law and a third man. By the light of a fire, they butchered the meat into the night and carried home a substantial supply of it.

Crockett continued to provision his family through the winter with game from the area. He hunted turkey and deer with success but was always on the lookout for bear.

Following a successful winter hunting season, Crockett rode to the town of Jackson in Madison County, some 40 miles away, to sell his hides, pelts, and bearskins. He traded them for staples such as coffee, sugar, and salt. While there, he went to a tavern to have a horn with some old friends from his soldiering days. In the tavern, he happened upon three politicians, including Dr. William E. Butler. One of the three suggested that Crockett run for the legislature again from his new district. Crockett declined, saying he was not interested. He then returned home to Rutherford Fork and thought nothing more of it.

In a week or two, a visitor stopped by Crockett's cabin and congratulated him on his candidacy. The visiting hunter produced a newspaper to prove his pronouncement. Crockett was shocked but soon grew just as determined to make whoever had played the trick pay for it dearly. He hired a man to work his farm in his stead and started electioneering.

Soon enough, Crockett's campaign forced the other three candidates to caucus and back only one of their number. The lot fell to Butler, whom Crockett wrote was a "clever fellow" and the "most talented man" he had ever run against.

On one occasion on the campaign trail, Crockett ran across Butler, who did not immediately recognize him until Crockett hailed him in front of a gathering. "Damn it, Crockett, is that you?" Butler said. Crockett replied, "Be sure it is, but I don't want it understood that I have come electioneering. I have just crept out of the cane, to see what discoveries I could make among the white folks." Crockett noted in his autobiography, "I told him that when I set out electioneering, I would go prepared to put every man on as good a footing when I left him as I found him on. I would therefore have me a large buckskin hunting-shirt made, with a couple of pockets holding about a peck each; and that in one I would carry a great big twist of tobacco, and in the other my bottle of liquor; for I knowed when I met a man and offered him a dram, he would throw out his quid of tobacco to take one, and after he had taken his horn, I would out with my twist, and give him another chew. And this way he would not be worse off than when I found him, and I would be sure to leave him in a first-rate good humor." Butler acknowledged that Crockett could out-campaign him. Crockett wrote, "I told him I would go on the products of the country; that I had industrious children, and the best of coon dogs; and they would hunt every night until midnight to support my election; and when the coon fur wasn't good, I would myself go a wolfing, and shoot down a wolf, and skin his head, and his scalp would be good to me for three dollars, in our State Treasury money; and this way I would get along on the big string." When Crockett finished his spiel, the crowd roared. Even Butler laughed. Crockett determined that he had won the favor of the people and would likely get their votes.

Crockett and Butler often appeared together on the campaign

trail to give voters a chance to hear their views back to back. It was customary in those days to make outlandish statements about one's opponent, then to socialize with him in the understanding that it was all acceptable. In this spirit, Butler once invited Crockett to his home. Being a wealthy man, Butler had a finely appointed home that included a luxurious rug that Crockett refused to step on. In fact, he spent the evening making a point to step around it. Later on the campaign trail, Crockett drew a pointed contrast between Butler's rug and the bearskin rugs on backwoods cabin floors: "Fellow citizens, my aristocratic competitor has a fine carpet, and every day he walks on truck finer that any gowns your wife or your daughters, in all their lives, ever wore."

Crockett worked to cast his opponent as a wealthy, privileged man living among backwoods pioneers. He had some success in that vein. He also tried to confuse and befuddle his opponent. During their campaigning together, Crockett usually spoke first and Butler followed. On one occasion after they had heard each other speak numerous times, Crockett asked if he might precede Butler. When Butler assented, Crockett rose and gave an almost flawless delivery of Butler's own speech. Butler then had to craft a new speech rather hurriedly.

Crockett won the election by 247 votes and thus was returned to the Tennessee General Assembly from a new district without missing a session (see the section on Murfreesboro, pages 29-37).

At the end of the second session of the 15th General Assembly in October 1824, Crockett returned to his home, which was now in the newly formed Gibson County. Given Crockett's popularity with his constituents, others saw an opportunity to unseat the current United States congressman from the Ninth Congressional District, Colonel Adam Alexander. In league with Henry Clay's economic strategy, Alexander had just voted for high tariffs, an unpopular position in the South. Pro-Jackson forces approached Crockett about running for Congress in 1825. He declined, saying later of the matter, "I couldn't stand that; it was a step above my knowledge, and I knowed nothing about Congress matters." Unfortunately, Crockett did not stay with his initial instincts. He eventually relented and ran for the congressional seat against Alexander.

In the campaign, Crockett hoped to capitalize on the outrage Southerners felt concerning the election of President John Quincy Adams over Andrew Jackson in August 1824. Jackson had won the popular vote, only to have the election thrown into the House of Representatives by the electoral college. There, Henry Clay countered the instructions from his Kentucky electorate and voted not for Jackson but for Adams. Adams was elected president, upon which he appointed Clay to serve as secretary of state. Despite the appearance of impropriety, none was ever proven. Still, the pro-Jackson forces in Tennessee were fighting the backers of Clay and Adams, of which Alexander was one. They thought Crockett, then an ardent Jackson supporter, could carry the day in claiming Alexander's congressional seat.

During the campaign, Crockett got a taste of the viciousness of national politics. Judge John Overton, who along with Andrew Jackson and James Winchester had founded Memphis in 1819, used the pen name Aristides to criticize Crockett's legislative record and to punish him for legislation he supported in opposition to large land speculators such as Overton himself.

Crockett lost the August 1825 election 52 percent to 48 percent, with fewer than 6,000 votes cast. He returned to his Obion River farm, where he resumed working, hunting, talking politics, and trying to find a way out of debt. The campaign had cost him dearly, and he needed a plan to make money. That was his impetus for getting into the business of manufacturing and shipping barrel staves.

In October after the failed campaign, Crockett hired some men to build two barges and to manufacture barrel staves from local timber. They built their craft on Obion Lake while Crockett wandered off from the project to engage in a bear hunt (see the next section on Reelfoot Lake State Park). During those months, Crockett killed 58 bears. Some suggest that number was the count for all who were in his party, not just Crockett alone. In either case, the hunt was remarkably successful. The meat provisioned Crockett's family and neighbors. He traded and sold the skins in Jackson. The tales of his bear-hunting skills brought additional acclaim to Crockett.

Returning to the lumber-and-boat project only on occasion and finally just before departure, Crockett was ill prepared for the journey. The party intended to float the craft down the Obion River, then down the Mississippi River to New Orleans. There, they planned to get a good price for the 30,000 staves and the lumber in the barges as well. It all seemed easy enough, but none of the men—and certainly not Crockett—was experienced with river craft. They did not test the boats before leaving, and they overloaded them as well. Disaster awaited them in the Memphis area (see the section on Memphis, pages 87-94).

Upon returning home from his failed lumber enterprise in the spring of 1826, Crockett went hunting for a month and killed 47 bears after they came out of hibernation. That brought the season's total to 105 kills. Over the summer, he also performed civic duties such as serving on a few juries of view, which supervised road construction from Trenton toward Dresden, toward Martin's Bluff, and from Rutherford to Obion County.

By the spring of 1827, Crockett was ready to campaign again. He began his second run for a seat in Congress from the Ninth Congressional District. The district included all the land west of the Tennessee River as it flowed north. It was divided into nine counties at the start of the election, but so many people moved into the area that by 1832—the year following Crockett's second term in Congress—the number of counties had doubled. (For information on Crockett's tenure in Congress from 1827 to 1831 and from 1833 to 1835, see the section on Washington, District of Columbia, pages 157-69.)

In advance of the election of 1831, Crockett sold some land and a young slave, Adeline, to his wife's brother, George Patton. Biographer James Shackford pointed out that beneath Crockett's signature on the deed and the bill of sale appeared for the first documented time the phrase, "Be always sure you are right, then go ahead." In August 1831, after losing his seat in Congress, Crockett remained at his home in the Obion River area. Soon afterward, he leased 20 acres in Weakley County adjacent to his land in Carroll County. He intended to clear the land and to improve his farm with a well, small cabins, a corncrib, and some fruit trees. By those means, he hoped to pay off some of his campaign debts. During the next two years, he also served on road juries and was sued for debt. Other than these scant accounts, little is known of this time except that Crockett was preparing to run again for Congress.

In the fall of 1833, after Crockett was reelected to Congress, his father-in-law, Robert Patton, died. Patton had moved from North Carolina to the Obion River area a few years earlier. Crockett and George Patton were made co-executors of the will. Two of Robert Patton's daughters and their husbands contested the will, which left each of them only $10. Co-executor George Patton did not reply in a timely fashion to Crockett's letters, so the administration of the will dragged on for a couple of years.

Crockett owned at least a couple of farms in the Obion River area. His wife, Elizabeth, and the children lived in Gibson County. However, when Crockett wrote letters from home, he did so from his Weakley County residence. It is interesting to note that no letters survive from David Crockett to his wife, though Crockett did write his children. Some historians have concluded that David and Elizabeth did not enjoy a close relationship and were estranged. Other historians decry that conclusion and suggest that the couple was no different from any other that had endured the trials and hardships they did over the years.

In July 1834, Crockett returned home to Tennessee from a trip to Philadelphia following the end of the spring session of Congress. As part of the Independence Day celebration Crockett attended in Philadelphia, the young Whigs presented him with great ceremony a custom-made ball-and-cap rifle (see the section on Philadelphia, Pennsylvania, pages 180-84). As with the other periods of his life between legislative sessions, little is known of Crockett's actions except through court records. In 1834, he appeared in court proceedings a few times regarding others' debts that he had secured. Despite his fame, Crockett continued to struggle financially.

Sometime in the fall before Crockett returned to Congress in mid-November 1834, his father, John Crockett, passed away, probably in the local community. David was made a co-administrator of his father's estate. By that time, he had already completed and published his autobiography. The timing of his father's death may explain why he never mentioned his father in his writings beyond the childhood episodes. By late November 1834, Crockett was back in Washington.

After a summer of campaigning to retain his seat in Congress, Crockett was defeated by 230 votes in August 1835 (see the section on Jackson, pages 56-62). Adam Huntsman would be the new congressman, and Crockett would find a new adventure. He was planning to explore opportunities in Texas.

Some papers relished publishing the news of Crockett's recent political defeat. The *Arkansas Gazette* referred to "the buffoon, Davy Crockett." The *Charleston Courier* played on Crockett's notoriety as "a lion" and suggested that he had been bested by "a Huntsman." Other papers portrayed Crockett in a better light.

During the three months between the lost election and Crockett's departure for Texas, he had some legal matters to handle. In October 1835, he was apparently completing the legal responses that would allow the will of his father-in-law, Robert Patton, to stand. On October 31, the day before his party of explorers left for Texas, Crockett wrote to his co-executor, George Patton. After explaining some of the details of the legal situation, he shared with Patton information about the party of four preparing to depart for Texas.

Going with Crockett would be his brother-in-law Abner Burgin, his wife's nephew William Patton (son of the deceased James Patton), and a neighbor, Lindsey K. Tinkle. They outfitted them-selves with horses, saddles, and guns. In the letter to George Patton, Crockett clearly expressed their intended route and objective: "We will go through Arkinsaw and I want to explore the Texes well before I return." According to biographer James Shackford, at the time of Crockett's departure from home, he had no intention of fighting for the independence of Texas. Historian Manley F. Cobia, Jr., writing nearly 50 years after Shackford, agreed with Shackford to a point but believed that Crockett became aware of the conflict in Texas along the way and then decided to join the fight.

On November 1, the party of four departed the Crockett home. From across the field, David turned and waved to his family, then

The Crockett museum in Rutherford has an interesting collection of frontier and farm artifacts and Crockett memorabilia.

Rebecca (or Rebekah) Hawkins Crockett's remains were reinterred at the replica cabin site.

rode beyond the trees. Some accounts suggest that Elizabeth declared audibly, and prophetically, that they would never see their father and husband again. Other accounts suggest that the party departed the area by steamboat to Memphis, though most historians concur that the men left on horseback. In any case, David Crockett's departure for Texas in the fall of 1835 was witnessed by that notorious harbinger of fate, Halley's comet, streaking through the West Tennessee night sky. (For more information, see the section on Memphis, pages 87-94.)

Reelfoot Lake was formed during the
New Madrid earthquake of 1811-12.

Reelfoot Lake State Park

Reelfoot Lake State Park is in Lake County in the north-
west corner of Tennessee. The visitor center, 2.5 miles east of
Tiptonville on TN 21, provides access to the lake and inter-
prets the natural and cultural history of the area. The 25,000-
acre lake offers hunting, fishing, pontoon-boat cruises, and
eagle watching.

The lake was formed during the New Madrid earthquake
of 1811-12. The land rose and fell, changing the landscape
and the water flow in the area. The land was marred by blow-
ing sand and deep fissures. Trees felled by high winds created
snarls of underbrush in which wildlife thrived and multiplied.
Traversing the land was difficult, but the hunting was excel-
lent. Crockett called the snarls of wind-felled trees and brush
"harracanes."

David Crockett lost the election of 1825, a campaign he reluctantly undertook to unseat the sitting United States congressman,

Colonel Adam Alexander. Following his first campaign loss, he returned home to Rutherford Fork of the Obion River. To help replenish his personal funds and pay off his campaign debts, he hired some men to build two barges and fill them with 30,000 barrel staves. He planned to sell the lot—staves and boats—in New Orleans after floating down the Mississippi River in a grand adventure. Work began in the fall of 1825 about 25 miles from Crockett's cabin, by his own estimate. Crockett worked at the project for a while but eventually felt the call of the wild and ventured off on several bear hunts during the late fall and winter while his hired men continued their labor.

In his first hunt, Crockett killed and salted down what he thought was enough bear meat to provision his family for the winter. A distant neighbor then called upon him to come hunt in his area, as the bears were "extremely fat," he said. "I knowed that when they were fat they were easily taken, for a fat bear can't run fast or long," Crockett wrote. "But I asked a bear no favors, no way, further than civility, for I now had eight large dogs, and as fierce as painters [panthers], so that a bear stood no chance at all to get away from them."

Crockett had great success in his outing with the neighbor, killing 15 bears. After a few days back at carpentry work, he was again eager to hunt. This time, he took his young son, probably Robert Patton Crockett, who was then about nine years old. They crossed the lake, killed three bears, then erected some poles on which to hang the meat to keep it from wolves. Another party of hunters soon happened upon Crockett, who told them to rest their dogs at his camp while he went after another bear. In short order, he scared up a beast that ran toward his camp and was set upon by the second party of hunters. Crockett let them have it while he set off in search of another.

His dogs soon scared up three more bears, all within 30 minutes. Crockett killed one with his knife without even firing his rifle. The dogs took off after another, but Crockett could not keep up with them through the snarls and fissures. He found out later that his dogs had treed a bear about five miles away. A man living nearby heard the ruckus and came out to shoot the bear. The dogs left the kill and returned to find Crockett awaiting them in camp.

Upon his return to camp, Crockett had come across a single laborer working in the woods to prepare a field. Crockett offered the man a good supply of bear meat if he would help salt down what Crockett and his son had already killed. The man eagerly joined them. By the end of the week-long hunt, between Christmas and New Year's, Crockett had killed 17 bears. He gave the man 1,000 pounds of bear meat, which the fellow was greatly pleased to have.

After the first of the year, Crockett went hunting with a neighbor named McDaniel, though he knew the bears would by then have "taken to house" for the winter. They found one bear in a hollow tree. Crockett's son busied himself with chopping down the tree while his father took the dogs a safe distance away. Looking back, Crockett saw the bear poke its head out of the hole. Awakened by the chopping, it was preparing to climb down the tree toward his son. Crockett called out a warning. McDaniel raised his gun and shot the bear as it came down the tree. "As soon as it touched the ground the dogs were all round it," Crockett wrote, "and they had a roll-and-tumble fight to the foot of the hill where they stopp'd him. I ran up, and putting my gun against the bear, fired and killed him."

Crockett's bear-hunting exploits continued through the winter. According to an editor in 1880, one particular tale surpassed anything ever written for "real peril and adventure." Crockett was following his dogs late in the day as they trailed a monstrous bear. He had to work hard to climb through the brush and over the rough ground. As he waded a couple of creeks, he found the cold water a little refreshing. By the time he caught up with his dogs, he could not see well in the moonless night. Still, he believed the bear was in the fork of the tree his dogs had surrounded. "At last," Crockett wrote, "I thought I could shoot by guess." He fired but apparently missed. The bear then climbed out on a limb where Crockett could see it a little better. He reloaded and fired again. The bear fell among the dogs and began to fight right at Crockett's feet. He occasionally glimpsed the white of a dog, but the bear's black fur made it indistinguishable in the darkness. Crockett pulled out his "butcher"—his hunting knife— and prepared to defend himself. The bear got down in one of the fissures created by the earthquake, the dogs at its head. Crockett poked his rifle into the bear and fired, hoping for a well-placed shot. However, he hit only the fleshy part of the leg. The bear crawled out of the hole and fought the dogs, which forced it back down again. Crockett could not locate his gun, having laid it down in the dark. He found a pole and began to poke the bear, trying to determine which part was where. From the sounds, he could tell his dogs had the head turned toward them. With that, Crockett jumped on the bear with his butcher drawn and felt around for the shoulders. He plunged the knife deep in the beast's back and struck the heart. It collapsed in the fissure. Crockett and his dogs crawled out.

Crockett then built a fire, which burned poorly. By that light, he dragged the bear carcass from the hole and butchered it. By that time, his wet clothes had become a problem. To stay warm, he started to holler and jump around. "But all this wouldn't do," Crockett wrote, "for my blood was now getting cold, and the chills coming all over me." To save his life, he found a good-sized tree without any limbs for thirty feet. He climbed the tree and, with his arms locked, slid down. "This would make the insides of my legs and arms feel mighty warm and good," he wrote. "I continued this till daylight in the morning, and how often I clumb up my tree and slid down I don't know, but I reckon at least a hundred times."

The next day, he found his son and McDaniel, who had feared him dead. They gathered their kills and prepared them for the trip home. In camp that night, they endured an earthquake. As Crockett wrote, it "shook the earth so, that we were rocked about like we had been in a cradle . . . and thought it might take a notion and swallow us up, like the big fish did Jonah."

Crockett's hunting party traveled 30 miles home to Rutherford Fork, having killed 58 bears that fall and winter. In mid-January, Crockett returned to help with work on his lumber enterprise. He set off with the barges in early February 1826 and returned by early spring. After the bears ended their hibernation, he again went hunting and killed another 47. The remarkable total of 105 bears killed in those few months enhanced the tales of the legendary hunting prowess of David Crockett.

Memphis

Located where I-40 crosses the Mississippi River in the southwest corner of Tennessee, Memphis is the largest city in the state and the economic capital of the mid-South. A historic marker on Front Street at Jackson Avenue commemorates the original river-front section of the city, an area now occupied by The Pyramid. On the southeast corner of the intersection is another historic marker. It honors Marcus Winchester, the first mayor of Memphis and David Crockett's political champion and financial backer.

Confederate Park, located on Front Street at Court Avenue five blocks south of Jackson Avenue, affords elevated views of the Mississippi River and Mud Island. A series of connected river-front parks—Tom Lee Park, Ashburn Park, and Martyr's Park—sit along South Riverside Boulevard south of Beale Street and offer broad vistas of the Mississippi. From any of these vantage points, one can imagine the power of the Mississippi confronted by Crockett and his boatmen on their way to New Orleans in 1826.

The Bell Tavern sat on North Front Street near its intersections with Overton Avenue and North Parkway, probably where The Pyramid is now located. The commemorative marker at the site was missing at the time of this writing. It said, "Across the street stood one of Memphis's famous hostelries, at which many notables stopped, and in which took place many events of historic interest. Here, in 1819, Andrew Jackson, James Winchester, and John Overton met, founded, and named the city of Memphis. David Crockett stopped here en route to Texas and his death at the Alamo."

The oldest parts of Memphis, which has thrived for two centuries as a river town, have been replaced by modern structures. Today, The Pyramid occupies the location of the city's original river-front buildings, which were abandoned as the business center moved south a short distance. One of the early river-front businesses was the shop of Marcus Winchester, who became Crockett's benefactor and political champion. Another site was the Bell Tavern, which some accounts say Crockett visited on his way west to explore Texas.

In early February 1826, Crockett was floating down the Mississippi River from the Obion River country intending to sell some lumber in New Orleans (see the section on Rutherford, pages 65-82). Just above Memphis, he and his ill-prepared crew ran into trouble.

Their success in floating their craft down the small, slow Obion River perhaps gave the men more confidence than was warranted. When they reached the Mississippi, they soon lost control of the barges. As the current swept them by other flatboats, experienced boatmen called out suggestions on what to do. Workers at landings along the way could immediately tell that Crockett's craft were in trouble and shouted advice. The barges were careening downriver at the mercy of the powerful current. Taking matters into his own hands, Crockett ordered the two boats lashed together. Now, they were one large block of wood tossed about at the whim of the river. Disgusted at his predicament, Crockett went into the cabin below, wishing he were hunting bear instead.

As the barges approached Memphis, the river divided around a set of islands known as Paddy's Hen-and-Chicks. (Paddy Meagher, associated with the area since 1783, had built a warehouse at Memphis in 1823.) At the head of Old Hen, huge trees ripped from the

The mighty Mississippi, which almost drowned Crockett, churns past Memphis.

What was the Memphis waterfront district in the 1820s is occupied today by The Pyramid.

banks upstream had become ensnarled in the sand bar. The current had stripped the limbs and bark. Those huge trees—a navigational hazard known as "sawyers"—bobbed violently in the current. They could easily rupture the hull of a boat or barge that got too close.

Unfortunately, Crockett's inexperienced boatmen allowed the lashed barges to get crosswise in the current. They smashed into a sawyer about 200 yards off the tip of Old Hen. The sawyer snagged the barges and began pulling them under. Crockett's barge, in the rear, nosed beneath the first one. The river poured in the rear boat's hatchway with such force that Crockett, still below decks at the moment of impact, was unable to escape the rapidly flooding cabin. As the barge pitched down, he climbed to the high point inside the cabin, where a hole had been cut for ease in scooping water from the river. That small hole was his only hope. Crockett tried to climb through but became wedged with only his arms and head sticking out. As he recalled years later, "I put my arms through and hollered as loud as I could roar, as the boat I was in hadn't yet quite filled with water up to my head, and the hands who were next to the raft, seeing my arms out, and hearing me holler, seized them, and began to pull. I told them I was sinking, and to pull my arms off, or force me through, for now I know'd well enough it was neck or nothing, come out or sink."

"By a violent effort," the men pulled, tearing from Crockett's body his shirt and trousers and a fair amount of skin. "I was literally skin'd like a rabbit," he wrote. No sooner had he been pulled free than the barge disappeared below the surface. A moment later, the other barge disappeared, too, as the men scrambled onto the debris and sawyers at Old Hen. The crew sat there all night nearly a mile from either bank, the completely naked Crockett shivering in the cold February air.

When daylight came, they hailed a passing boat, which sent a skiff to retrieve them. Some accounts say the boat came upriver from Memphis just for them. The boat carried the party of barefooted and bareheaded men and the still-naked Crockett to Memphis, where a merchant took them into his care and provided them clothing, shoes, and hats. The merchant was Major Marcus Winchester, the son of James Winchester, for whom the town where Crockett mustered for the Creek War was named. The younger Winchester had in 1819 become the first merchant in Memphis and was also its first mayor. He brought the river refugees to his

A naked and nearly drowned Crockett was taken in and clothed by Marcus Winchester at his store in 1826.

home, where his wife, Mary, fed them a welcomed meal. Later, as word of the men's adventure spread about town, Crockett entertained a crowd in the tavern with tall tales and stories of his adventures. He also joined the men in drinking.

Crockett was no stranger to the residents of Memphis, as the town was in the Ninth Congressional District, and he had just run for that seat in August. Seeing how well the people took to Crockett, Winchester encouraged him to remain in politics. He also offered his financial support.

From Memphis, Crockett and one member of his party took a boat downriver to Natchez to try to find the barges or learn their fate. They heard that some men had tried unsuccessfully to salvage one of the barges. Crockett subsequently returned to his home in Rutherford in 1826 with nothing to show for his investment.

Following his election defeat in August 1835 to retain his congressional seat, Crockett decided to explore Texas (see the section on Rutherford, pages 65-82). He, two family members, and a neighbor left Gibson County on November 1, 1835. They hoped to explore the land and make their fortunes in Texas.

Most historic accounts suggest that Crockett and his party went directly to Memphis from Gibson County, but Manley F. Cobia, Jr., wrote in 2003 that they rode first to Jackson and then to Bolivar. In those communities, Crockett may have first heard about the revolution in Texas and may have changed his plans. According to one of Cobia's sources, Crockett left Jackson with "30 men well armed and equipped." They rode to Bolivar, where Crockett spent the night and received the next day "a hero's send-off." From Bolivar, the men stopped next in Memphis. Perhaps some of the large party went another way toward Texas, or perhaps they turned back. In any case, only a few men arrived with Crockett in Memphis.

Crockett stayed at the City Hotel. In a farewell party they

gave for themselves, the men reportedly enjoyed themselves to excess. They visited many local taverns, which were not bawdy Western-style saloons but commodious drinking establishments that attracted well-to-do persons, among others. The travelers began their celebration at the Union Hotel after some of Crockett's friends saw him in the street. A dozen revelers departed the Union Hotel without taking any drinks because the room was too small. They retired to Hart's Saloon, which was also a drugstore and bakery. When the proprietor demanded payment after every drink, the party moved to McCool's, which was mostly a dry-goods store that was kept quite clean and tidy. The revelers hoisted Crockett on their shoulders and dropped him feet-first on the counter, which the proprietor had just covered with a clean oilcloth. Crockett was asked to make a toast. It was then that he declared the famous words recorded by historian James D. Davis, who was then 16 years old and living in Memphis. Reflecting on his recent political defeat (at the hands of peglegged Adam Huntsman) and his new adventure, Crockett, his drink raised in the air, said, "Since you have chosen to elect a man with a timber toe to succeed me, you may all go to hell and I will go to Texas."

As engaging as that story is, it should be noted that historian Davis penned it as much as 30 years after the fact. Some writers have suggested that he was more interested in telling a good tale than in recording an account of the evening. In any case, the sentiment, however expressed, was appropriately "Crockettesque." History records that he repeated the sentiment many times over the following few months.

As the proprietor brooded over the treatment the rowdy customers were giving his establishment, he made an offhand remark to one of the party. Someone threw something, and a fight broke out. When people began jumping over the bar,

McCool ran the patrons out without collecting any payment for the drinks. The revelers, not wanting to end the evening in such fashion, retired to Jo Cooper's place, where the wholesaler provided them free-of-charge drinks from his wide assortment of libations. The party continued into the night, Crockett providing speeches and stories.

In the morning, the travelers boarded a ferry to cross the Mississippi River. Historian Davis wrote his personal recollection of Crockett on seeing the party leave: "He wore that same veritable coon-skin cap and hunting shirt, bearing upon his shoulder his ever faithful rifle. No other equipment, save his shot-pouch and powder-horn, do I remember seeing."

Some historians have concluded that Crockett's party took a steamboat down the Mississippi to the Arkansas River, then upstream to Little Rock. According to Cobia, the ferryman delivered the party to the west bank of the river, where the riders took the military road 135 miles to Little Rock (see the section on Little Rock, Arkansas, pages 185-89).

In 1813, volunteers from Winchester rode to Beaty's Spring (now Brahan Springs), where General Andrew Jackson's troops joined them.

ALABAMA

Huntsville

Huntsville is located in Madison County in extreme north-central Alabama between the Tennessee River and the Tennessee state line at the intersection of US 231 and US 72.

Beaty's Spring is today known as Brahan Springs. Brahan Springs Park and its series of lakes are in West Huntsville on Drake Avenue at Ivey Avenue 0.7 mile west of US 231. The park is home to monuments honoring the veterans of 20th-century conflicts, but no mention is made of the 19th-century Creek War.

Ditto's Landing, a public park along the Tennessee River at Whitesburg, is operated by the Huntsville-Madison County Marina and Port Authority. It is located off US 231 eight miles south of Drake Avenue and 0.8 mile east of US 231 on Hobbs Island Road (not to be confused with Hobbs Road, which

On August 30, 1813, following an unprovoked attack by frontier militia on a party of Creek Indians at Burnt Corn Creek, a force of 1,000 Creek warriors—called Red Sticks by white settlers, and led by Peter McQueen and Red Eagle (William Weatherford)—massacred soldiers and settlers at Fort Mims. The following month, David Crockett and his fellow mounted militia volunteers left Winchester, Tennessee, to fight the Red Sticks. They rode south toward the Tennessee River and beyond Huntsville to Beaty's Spring. The men mustered there with other companies that had responded to the call for volunteers. Captain Robert Beaty had bought the land and springs in 1809. General Andrew Jackson paid Beaty for wagons, feed for the officers' horses, and damage done to his fences by the encampment. Beaty later sold the land in 1818 to John Brahan.

Crockett described the approximately 1,300 men who mustered at Beaty's Spring as "all mounted volunteers, and all determined to fight." They were men "of the real grit." As for himself, he said he "felt wolfish all over." The men had actually responded to the local call before General Andrew Jackson had received word of the massacre at Fort Mims. They planned to await Jackson's arrival, but they would not wait for long.

Major John H. Gibson, for whom Gibson County, Tennessee, was later named, wanted some volunteers to help him scout the area across the river. Captain Francis Jones recommended Crockett, who in turn recommended a partner of his own choosing. He selected George Russell, the young son of Major William Russell of Winchester. Major Gibson was not impressed with Russell because "he hadn't beard enough to please him," said Crockett in his autobiography. "I know'd George Russel, and I know'd there was no mistake in him; and I didn't think that courage ought to be measured by the beard for fear a goat would have the preference over a man." Crockett, Russell, Gibson, and the others prepared for their morning departure as scouts.

The party of 13 horsemen crossed the Tennessee River at Ditto's Landing and entered Creek land. At their first camp, the volunteers divided into two parties. Gibson took six men with him, while Crockett took five. The parties separated with plans to rendezvous, but Gibson did not arrive at the appointed spot. After waiting until the following morning, Crockett declared that he had come to search the area and would not return until he had done that. He and his men rode on.

After a while, they came upon the cabin of a man named Radcliff, a white settler whose wife was a Creek. They lived on the edge of the Creek Nation. Radcliff fed the men and let them water their horses, but he seemed nervous all the time Crockett

Crockett and the rest of Andrew Jackson's army crossed the Tennessee River at Ditto's Landing, a ferry service established in 1807 by James Ditto.

was there. He finally declared that a party of 10 Creek warriors had come by his home just an hour earlier. Radcliff feared that if they returned and found the militiamen receiving hospitality from him, they would kill him and his family.

Crockett and his party mounted their horses and rode toward a village of friendly Creeks some eight miles away. Along the way, they happened upon two black slaves, brothers, riding Indian ponies and carrying good guns. They had been captured by the Creeks but had escaped and were, Crockett said, "trying to get back to their masters again." Crockett sent one of them on alone to Ditto's Landing but kept the other with him because he "could talk Indian."

The party of militiamen arrived at the Creek village on October 6, 1813. It contained about 40 inhabitants. While the black interpreter talked to the Indians, Crockett amused himself by joining the young boys of the village at shooting arrows at targets by the light of pine torches. The villagers were anxious, the interpreter reported to Crockett, for the same reason Radcliff had given. They feared that the Red Sticks—the warring tribes of Creeks would find the militiamen at the village and would destroy them all. Crockett instructed the interpreter to tell them "that I would watch, and if one would come that night, I would carry the skin of his head home to make me a moccasin." The villagers laughed, and then everyone retired for the evening. The militiamen slept with their guns in their arms.

As the village quieted, "I heard the sharpest scream that ever escaped the throat of a human creature," Crockett reported. "It was more like a wrathy painter [panther]." The scream came from a Creek who was returning to the village. The interpreter learned from him that a large war party had been seen crossing the Coosa

River at Ten Islands. The war party was believed to be headed to fight Jackson.

Crockett felt compelled to report this news immediately. He and his men mounted their horses and covered the 65 miles back to Beaty's Spring by the light of a near-full moon, riding all night and into the next morning, October 7. At midmorning, Crockett reported his news directly to Colonel John Coffee, who did not pay much attention. However, when Major Gibson returned the next day with substantially the same report, "this seemed to put our colonel all in a fidget," Crockett recalled. He concluded that his word as a private was worthless and that officers believed only other officers. This irked him greatly and affected his attitude for the rest of his life about people of rank, especially those in the military.

Meanwhile, Coffee ordered some breastworks built and sent a messenger to Fayetteville with word for General Jackson. Coffee requested Jackson to "push on like the very mischief, for fear we should all be cooked up to a cracklin before they could get there," Crockett wrote. Jackson's soldiers arrived the next day after a forced march. Jackson ordered Coffee to cross the Tennessee River and search out Creek villages and camps along the Black Warrior River. (For more information, see the section on Tuscaloosa, pages 115-21.)

Crockett wrote that he stood up to General Andrew Jackson at Fort Strother.

Ohatchee

A historic marker for Fort Strother is on AL 144 some 1.7 miles west of AL 77 near Ohatchee in Calhoun County, northwest of Anniston. The marker, located at AL 144 and Valley Drive, is a quarter-mile west of the dam that impounds the Coosa River. AL 144 crosses the dam.

On the west side of the dam, a road leads to the administrative building and the Ten Islands Boat Ramp overlooking the historic area known as Ten Islands. The site is submerged by H. Neely Henry Lake.

During the Creek War, David Crockett and other militiamen under Colonel John Coffee pillaged and burned Black Warrior Town, located along the Black Warrior River. Afterward, Coffee's men returned northeast and joined Andrew Jackson's forces, which had crossed at Ditto's Landing and marched upriver three miles to camp opposite the upper end of Hobb's Island. After resting there awhile, the army marched farther up the Tennessee River to Thompson's Creek (known today as Honeycomb Creek, which flows into Gunthersville Lake just above Gunthersville Dam). There in late October, Jackson established a supply depot called Fort Deposit (or Deposite), not to be confused with the fort of the same name built later by Jackson south of what is now Montgomery. He ordered supplies to be delivered to this site downriver from East Tennessee, but the contractors failed to meet their obligations.

Crockett and a small group of militiamen had previously come upon the cabin of a white settler named Radcliff, who lived with his Creek wife at the boundary of the Creek Nation (see the section on Huntsville, pages 95-99). Now, when Jackson's forces reached the same home, they found that Radcliff had hidden all his provisions. They also learned that it was Radcliff who had sent a Creek warrior into the nearby village screaming a war cry and warning falsely of the amassing of a Creek war party. Radcliff had simply wanted Crockett's armed militia out of the area. In fact, no large party of Creeks was advancing north and seeking to destroy General Jackson and his army. As punishment for concocting the hoax, the army conscripted Radcliff's two sons and forced them into service as interpreters.

Jackson intended to march down the Coosa River to its junction with the Tallapoosa River in the heart of the Red Stick country near what is now Montgomery. As he advanced, he planned to erect forts to protect his rear and to provide provisions for the advancing army. One step toward this goal was to march toward Ten Islands on the Coosa and to build Fort Strother. Turning south from Thompson's Creek, Jackson marched Crockett and the rest of his men overland and across some rough, hilly terrain. They made camp at Wills Creek, probably at the Coosa River opposite what is now Gadsden. The site has since been inundated by H. Neely Henry Lake. It was there that Colonel Coffee was promoted to general.

From Camp Wills, the men were divided into search parties to forage for provisions. "We then marched to the Ten Islands, on the Coosa river," wrote Crockett, "where we [later] established a fort, and our spy companies were sent out." It was in this way that Jackson learned about the village of Tallasehatchee. He sent Coffee there with 1,000 men, including Crockett. They forded the Coosa River at the Fish Dams, four miles above Ten Islands. Five hundred men attacked, while 500 protected the rear. Coffee's soldiers then proceeded to massacre the inhabitants of the Creek village (see the next section on Tallasehatchee).

Afterward, the men marched to Ten Islands. Jackson's troops joined them there from Camp Wills. Together, they built Fort Strother. The stockade fort was 100 yards square with blockhouses. Eventually, it contained a supply warehouse, eight hospital huts, 25 tents, and some hogpens.

Within four days of arriving at Ten Islands, they received word that a party of friendly Creeks was trapped at Fort Talladega (Lashley's Fort) by hostile Creeks holding them in a siege. Crockett subsequently participated in the victory there (see the section on Talladega, pages 109-12).

Following the action at Talladega, General Jackson was outraged that he could not advance. Not only was he without provisions, but Generals James White and John Cocke, his political rivals, had refused to bring their Tennessee militiamen to protect Jackson's rear as he advanced down the Coosa River. Under the circumstances, Jackson returned to Fort Strother. "We now remained at the fort a few days," Crockett wrote, "but no provision came yet, and we were all likely to perish. The weather also began to get very cold; and our clothes were nearly worn out, and horses getting very feeble and poor."

Crockett made history at that time. Well known in his command for being something of a troublemaker, he was insubordinate to his officers on occasion. One of them, a captain who described Crockett as "a private, an awkward, boy-like soldier," advised Crockett that he was taking the matter of insubordination to General Jackson. Crockett supposedly said he wanted to come along to hear what the general had to say. After being presented with the situation, the general replied to the captain in rather formal terms: "Don't you make any orders on your men without maturing them, and then you execute them, no matter what the cost." Upon Crockett's return to his company, some of the men asked what the general had said. Crockett replied, "The old general told the captain to be sure he was right, then go ahead." Thus was born the aphorism that Crockett proudly proclaimed throughout his life. Some accounts ascribe the phrase to others whom Crockett then copied. In any case, it was Crockett who made famous the declaration, "Be always sure you're right, then go ahead."

Around that same time, the volunteers began to get restless. They believed they had served their time—60 days, according to Crockett—and they were ready to leave. In his autobiography, Crockett told a remarkable account of how he and the volunteers loaded and primed their rifles and walked across the bridge, despite Jackson's order that a cannon be aimed and readied for firing at anyone who crossed. Crockett wrote that Jackson said they were "the damned'st volunteers he had ever seen in his life: that we would volunteer and go out and fight, and then at our pleasure would volunteer and go home again in spite of the devil."

Unfortunately, as James Shackford pointed out in his Crockett biography, the events never happened as Crockett wrote them. Indeed, there was significant grumbling among the troops, along with several threats of a mutiny and more than a few attempts. But General Andrew Jackson was the hero, not Crockett. When an entire brigade was preparing to walk off to Tennessee, Jackson sat on his horse at the end of the bridge with an old musket he had hurriedly grabbed. Because he was nursing a wound to his arm—a wound suffered in a duel—Jackson propped the firearm on his horse's neck and pointed it at the mutineers. The parties glared at each other for a long while. No one challenged the determination that showed in Jackson's eyes. He stared down the volunteers almost single-handedly. None left. Some accounts say it was afterwards determined that the old musket probably would not have fired. Later, when another brigade threatened to depart, Jackson had the artillery prepare to fire into any parties moving toward home. Again, his determination prevailed.

Contrary to the account of the episode presented in his autobiography, Crockett was not among the first group of would-be deserters. They were all infantry. Crockett and the other mounted volunteers had already been released on furlough to rest their horses. They reported back on December 8. And according to Shackford, the muster rolls reported that Crockett served out his 90 days—not 60—and was discharged on December 24.

It appears that in 1834, Crockett fabricated the entire episode in his autobiography for his political advantage. The events as he wrote them some 20 years later showed common men—and himself in particular—standing up to Jackson, Crockett's political rival at the time. Moreover, the story as Crockett wrote it was laced liberally with references to Crockett's plans, should he be elected president, to replace the federal deposits Jackson had removed from the Second United States Bank while Congress was recessed.

Though Crockett served his entire 90 days and knew well that was the time for which he had enlisted, he had to claim an enlistment of 60 days to make the timing of his story work. Crockett's suggestion that he deserted caused rumors and actually served to impugn his reputation.

Almost unbelievably, another David Crockett, also from Tennessee, fought in the Creek War and did in fact desert. Consequently, one can find an official record that shows a deserter named David Crockett, but it was a different soul, not Tennessee's frontier hero.

Crockett's service ended in December 1813, notwithstanding his wholesale fabrication of service throughout 1814 in other battles. Crockett simply was not present at the Battles of Emuckfaw and Horseshoe Bend, though he apparently felt he needed the image of extensive military service for his presidential campaign.

Crockett returned home to his family on Bean's Creek around Christmas and presumably resumed the life of a frontier farmer. However, when the call for volunteers came again in August 1814, he reenlisted for another tour of duty in the Creek War (see the section on Fort Mims, pages 121-28).

Tallasehatchee

The actual site of the village of Tallasehatchee is unknown today, though it is believed by historians and archaeologists to lie in Calhoun County northwest of Anniston along Tallasseehatchee Creek between AL 77 and US 431 near AL 144. The name of the site is spelled at least four different ways. Three markers in the area commemorate the events here. A state highway historic marker is located along US 431 some 2.5 miles north of AL 144 at the Tallasseehatchee Creek bridge. A marker erected by the Daughters of the American Revolution commemorating "Tallasahatchie" and a monument to Lincoyer (or Lyncoya) are located a quarter-mile along McCullars Lane off AL 144. The Lincoyer marker uses the historic name Talluschatches and the modern name Tallasehatchee. McCullars Lane is 0.6 mile west of US 431 along AL 144. The markers are about eight miles east of the Fort Strother marker on AL 144.

Tallasehatchee was the site of a horrific massacre of American Indians by an army of 1,000 soldiers, volunteers, and militia under the command of General John Coffee, operating under orders from General Andrew Jackson. David Crockett participated in the slaughter, which at the time was hailed as retribution for the massacre at Fort Mims on August 30, 1813.

While Jackson's army was building Fort Strother, its scouts captured some Creek warriors and their leader, Bob Catala. The scouts also reported finding a hostile Creek village about eight miles (some accounts say 13 miles) to the east. Jackson ordered General Coffee to destroy the village. Crockett and the rest of Coffee's men mounted up and followed two friendly Creeks toward the village. Accompanying the troops were some Cherokee warriors under the leadership of Dick Brown.

On November 3, 1813, Coffee's force encircled the town without being spied. Captain Hammond's rangers than advanced. When the Creeks saw them, they sent up a yell. The warriors then ran out of the town toward the advancing soldiers. Jackson's forces fired first, and the warriors returned fire. The troops closed their formation around the town, assuring that no one could escape.

The villagers surrendered, according to Crockett. The women

came out and clung to the soldiers, seeking mercy for the village. Amidst this, Crockett and others saw some warriors (Crockett counted 46) run into a house. When the men were inside, a Creek woman lay on the ground outside, used her feet to pull a bow, and let fly one arrow. It hit and killed a Lieutenant Moore. Crockett wrote that this was the first person he had ever seen killed by an arrow.

The soldiers were enraged. The woman "was fired on, and had at least twenty balls blown through her," Crockett wrote. After that, the massacre began. "We shot them like dogs," Crockett recorded. The soldiers set the house on fire and burned it down with the 46 warriors inside. Crockett reported seeing a young boy of perhaps 12 crawling on the ground near the burning house with an arm and thigh broken from being shot. "He was so near the burning house that the grease was stewing out of him." Crockett noted that the boy crawled without making a sound of distress or asking for mercy.

According to Crockett, 186 Creeks—men, women, and children—either died or were taken prisoner. Other accounts say that 186 male warriors died and that 84 women and children were taken

Monuments recall the soldiers' massacre of villagers at Tallasehatchee.

prisoner. Five of Coffee's soldiers died, and 18 (some accounts say 41) were wounded. After the massacre, Jackson wrote a letter to Tennessee governor Willie Blount declaring, "We have retaliated for the destruction of Fort Mims."

The slaughter was extensive but not complete. On the battlefield, a 10-month-old infant was found in the grasp of his dead mother's arms. The child was brought to Jackson along with all the prisoners. Jackson encouraged the Creek prisoners to take care of the child, but they replied that since all the child's relatives were dead, the baby should be killed, too. Refusing to consider such a notion, Jackson took the child into his personal care. After reviving the infant in his tent with brown sugar dissolved in water, he sent him to his home at The Hermitage. That boy, Lincoyer, subsequently lived as a member of the Jackson family. He favored his Creek ways and was often visited in later years by members of his tribe. Though he ran away several times, he was embraced and loved by Andrew Jackson and his wife, Rachel, as family. In July 1828, as Jackson was campaigning for president, his teenage son Lincoyer contracted tuberculosis and died. In December, after the election, Rachel Jackson died also.

The victorious army marched from Tallasehatchee back toward Ten Islands. Upon arriving at Fort Strother, which was then under construction, they discovered that no supplies had yet reached the site. The men had been on half-rations for several days and were hungry. They thus returned to the scene of the massacre to see what might be there.

The soldiers walked into the town, where the bodies of those they had killed were quite visible. "They looked very awful," Crockett wrote, "for the burning had not entirely consumed them, but given them a terrible appearance." Lieutenant Richard Call later wrote, "We found as many as eight or ten dead bodies in a single cabin. Some of the cabins had taken fire, and half consumed bodies were seen amidst the smoking ruins. In other instances dogs had torn and feasted on the mangled bodies of their masters."

The soldiers soon discovered some potatoes in the cellar beneath the house in which they had burned the warriors. "Hunger compelled us to eat them," Crockett recounted, "though I had a little rather not, if I could have helped it, for the oil of the Indians we had burned up on the day before, had run down on them, and they looked like they had been stewed with fat meat." Crockett and the other soldiers ate the potatoes anyway. Some historians have suggested this act approached cannibalism.

Afterward, the men returned to Ten Islands and completed the building of Fort Strother. (For more information, see the section on Ohatchee, pages 100-105.)

Talladega

Talladega, the county seat of Talladega County, is located at the intersection of AI 21 (Battle Street) and AL 77. A historic marker for the Battle of Talladega sits on Battle Street on the lawn of the county courthouse. The Battle of Talladega monument is one block west on Battle Street at Spring Street. This elaborate domed monument has a fountain and four plaques. The adjacent markers commemorate additional historic events.

On November 3, 1813, a force of 1,000 men under General John Coffee massacred the inhabitants of the Creek village of Tallasehatchee. Following that, many Creek villages changed their allegiance. Having seen the total destruction pursued by Jackson's army, they feared him more than the threats of Red Eagle, who warned them of retribution if they did not join the Red Stick alliance. One such village was Talladega, which counted about 150 residents. The inhabitants took protection inside the fortification they called Lashley's (or Leslie's) Fort.

The hostile Red Sticks completely surrounded Lashley's Fort in Talladega. They warned the turncoat Creeks that if they did not join in an attack on Jackson, their fort would be plundered, their provisions would be taken, and they would all be killed. The inhabitants asked for three days to consider. This was a stalling tactic. Since no one could escape the siege to seek help, a brave warrior decided to try his hand at deception. He covered himself with the skin of a large hog, complete with head and feet. Crouching, he ambled his way out of the fort, rooting and grunting in plain view of the hostile camp. When he was a safe distance away, he leaped up, discarded his disguise, and ran to Fort Strother to ask for Jackson's assistance. "At length," wrote Crockett, "an Indian came to our guard one night, and hollered, and said he wanted to see 'Captain Jackson.'"

Hearing from the exhausted runner of the inhabitants' plight, Jackson ordered his men to prepare to leave camp about midnight.

The monument commemorating the Battle of Talladega recounts the rescue of friendly Creeks besieged by Red Sticks.

"In an hour we were all ready, and took up the line of march," wrote Crockett. They forded the Coosa River where it was 600 yards wide, each rider carrying a foot soldier behind him. That evening, they made camp within six miles of Talladega. Leaving at four o'clock on the morning of November 9, 1813, Jackson's army of 1,200 foot soldiers and 800 horsemen surrounded the 1,080 hostile Creeks, who in turn surrounded Lashley's Fort. "It was about an hour by the sun in the morning when we got near the fort," wrote Crockett. "We were piloted by friendly Indians and divided as we had done on a former occasion, so as to go to the right and left of the fort, and consequently, of the warriors who were camped near it."

Hoping to repeat the military maneuver they had employed at Tallasehatchee, Jackson's men began to close the square. "We then sent on old Major Russel [William Russell] with his spy company, to bring on the battle," wrote Crockett. Upon seeing this advance, the Red Sticks came running, firing after the decoys. "They were all painted as red as scarlet," wrote Crockett, "and were just as naked as they were born. . . .The Indians . . . came rushing forth like a cloud of Egyptian locusts, and screaming like all the young devils had been turned loose, with the old devil of all at their head." The Red Sticks chased the retreating party into the trap. The army closed around them and fired point-blank at the Red Sticks, who had no place to retreat. Crockett described the battle as the army surrounded the enemy: "They then broke like a gang of steers, and ran across to the other line, where they were again fired on; and so we kept them running from one line to the other, constantly under a heavy fire, till we had killed upwards of four hundred of them. They fought with guns, and also with bows and arrows."

To Jackson's dismay, in the heat of battle, a band of drafted militiamen broke into retreat or misunderstood orders, leaving a hole in the line. About 700 Red Sticks escaped. Except for that tactical error, Jackson believed he might have ended the Creek War much sooner.

After the battle, Crockett and the rest of Jackson's men counted 299 victims among the Red Sticks. The United States Army had lost 17 men. The soldiers, volunteers, and militia returned to Fort Strother carrying their 85 wounded in litters made of hides. The men had been hungry when they left Fort Strother on this campaign. On their return, they hoped to find that their promised provisions had arrived. Crockett and the others were soon disappointed. (For more information, see the section on Ohatchee, pages 100-105.)

Sylacauga

Sylacauga lies at the junction of US 280 and AL 21 southeast of Birmingham. Fort Williams, a supply depot and hospital during the Creek War, was located along the Coosa River at Cedar Creek about 12 miles west-southwest of Sylacauga near Talladega Springs. A historic marker commemorating the fort is on US 231 south of Sylacauga. Nearby Fayetteville was named by Tennessee volunteers for their home community. These settlers came to the area after the Creek War, having passed through it during the conflict.

Fort Decatur is not marked on the ground. It was located near what is now Milstead on the Tallapoosa River. AL 229, accessible at Exit 26 off I-85, crosses the Tallapoosa River near the site of the fort.

David Crockett scouted and hunted for his fellow soldiers as they marched across what is now southeast Alabama in the latter days of the Creek War. The men nearly starved for lack of provisions. Crockett's hunting expeditions helped bring in some game.

Having completed their search for hostile Creeks in the Apalachicola region (see the section on Pensacola, Florida, pages 129-33), Crockett and Major William Russell's men marched northwest toward Fort Decatur. The company's provisions had long been exhausted, and the men were constantly hungry. Each day as they marched, Crockett and other skilled hunters went out looking for game. "I hunted every day, and would kill every hawk, bird, or squirrel that I could find," wrote Crockett. At night, they threw everything into a pile and divided it among the men. "We know'd that nothing more could happen to us if we went than if we staid," Crockett wrote, "for it looked like it was to be starvation any way; we therefore determined to go on the old saying, root hog or die."

Over the next several days, Crockett ventured out each morning in hopes of finding game, no matter how small. "I found a squirrel, which I shot," he recalled, "but he got into a hole in the tree. The game was small, but necessity is not very particular; so I thought I must have him, and I climbed that tree thirty feet high, without a limb, and pulled him out of his hole." The hunters also flushed a covey of wild turkeys and shot a few of those. "I now began to think we had struck a breeze of luck, and almost forgot our past suffering to eat," wrote Crockett. He and his hunting companion had begun to cook up a stew when two of their party who had been sent ahead to get provisions came by with a sack of flour. They gave Crockett and his companion a cup each, which they used to thicken their stew. Crockett fed the men, then told them to hurry on to the main camp. When they arrived, they discovered that Captain William Russell, son of the major, was just about to shoot his horse to feed his men. Their timely arrival spared the animal's life.

Fourteen miles from Fort Decatur, Crockett killed a large buck, which the army cooked immediately. Crockett pushed on ahead to Fort Decatur but found that the men there had no bread and only one ration of meat they could provide. He then made his way across the river to what he called the "Big Warrior's Town." He eventually traded 10 bullets and 10 charges of powder for two hatfuls of corn, which he carried back to the soldiers.

These meager rations staved off starvation only for the moment. "Parched corn, and but little even of that, was our daily subsistence," Crockett wrote. The men were still nearly 50 miles from Fort Williams, where they hoped to get more food. However, when they reached that fort, they received only one ration of pork and one of flour. They then set out for Fort Strother, almost 40 miles away. "The horses were now giving out," Crockett wrote, "and I remember to have seen thirteen good horses left in one day, the saddles and bridles being thrown away."

On the way to Fort Strother, the army passed through the area of its battle with the Red Sticks at Lashley's Fort at Talladega. "We went through the old battle ground," Crockett recalled, "and it looked like a great gourd patch; the skulls of the Indians who were killed, still lay scattered all about, and many of their frames were still perfect, as the bones had not separated." While in the area, Crockett traded more bullets and powder for corn, which he shared with the men.

The next morning, Crockett was greeted by troops from East Tennessee who were heading to Mobile. Crockett's youngest brother, John, was with them. Crockett was given corn for himself and his horse. He stayed the night visiting. Meanwhile, the rest of the nearly starved men under Major Russell crossed the Coosa River and entered Fort Strother. There, they were fed adequately for the first time in weeks.

Crockett rested a few days at Fort Strother, then headed home to Bean's Creek. "Nothing more worthy of the reader's attention, transpired til I was safely landed at home once more with my wife and children," he wrote. (For more information, see the section on Maxwell, Tennessee, pages 41-46.)

Crockett identified Tuscaloosa as the site of Black Warrior Town along the Black Warrior River.

Tuscaloosa

Tuscaloosa is in Tuscaloosa County in west-central Alabama on I-20/I-59 at the junction with US 82. A historic marker for Black Warrior Town previously stood on US 11/US 43 across from Stillman College in the west part of Tuscaloosa. It referred to land adjacent to the Oliver Lock and Dam, located about a half-mile north of the college. The marker read, "Black Warrior's Town—One-half mile north was the Creek Indian village known as Black Warrior's Town, of which Oce-Oche-Motla was chief. After Tecumseh's visit in 1811, these Indians became hostile to white settlers. In 1812 Little Warrior brought Mrs. Martha C. Crawley of Tennessee to this Indian Village as a captive. She was rescued by Tandy Walker, a blacksmith, and taken to St. Stephens. This was one of the incidents which led to the Creek War. The village was destroyed in October 1813 by Colonel John Coffee and his Tennessee volunteers, one of whom was Davy Crockett." Visitors can experience the Black Warrior River and its history along the Tuscaloosa-Warrior River Walk, accessible at the foot of Greensboro Avenue north of University Boulevard.

The confluence of Sipsey Fork and Mulberry Fork of the Black Warrior River, an unmarked site, lies on CR 22 two miles east of Sipsey in Walker County. This location, about 50 miles north-northeast of Tuscaloosa, is believed by some to be the historic site of Black Warrior Town.

In his account of his Creek War experiences, David Crockett recorded that Colonel John Coffee's force, of which he was a part, burned Black Warrior Town. Crockett said the site was near Tuscaloosa, a town founded a few years after the attack but one that was already prominent by the time Crockett wrote his autobiography in the early 1830s. The geographic accuracy of Crockett's claim has been challenged. Some believe that Black Warrior Town was farther upstream at the confluence of Sipsey Fork and Mulberry Fork, not at Tuscaloosa. Still, Crockett named Tuscaloosa as the site.

General Andrew Jackson sent a force of 800 men across the Tennessee River. This party advanced under the command of Colonel Coffee. The men crossed at Muscle Shoals at a place Crockett called Melton Bluff. That cliff is in Lawrence County on the south bank three miles upstream from the convergence of the Lauderdale, Lawrence, and Limestone county lines at the mouth of Elk Creek. The Tennessee River was two miles wide there. Some of the men lost their horses in the crossing when the animals' feet became lodged in rock crevices on the river bottom.

The soldiers were ordered to explore the area around the Black Warrior and Etomb-iga-by (Tombigbee) rivers. They marched a great distance—perhaps 100 miles—downstream. The advancing army scared off Creek inhabitants. The soldiers entered the recently abandoned Black Warrior Town and pillaged it for supplies, taking corn and dried beans; one account says they made off with 300 bushels of corn. As they left, they burned the town, ostensibly to retaliate for the abduction of Martha Crawley (or Crowley) from the Duck River area of Tennessee in 1812. She had subsequently been rescued from Black Warrior Town, where she had been taken as a prisoner by Little Warrior.

After burning Black Warrior Town, Colonel Coffee's men turned northeast and marched back to Ditto's Landing. Despite their recent plundering, the army of 800 found itself without meat. Crockett asked for and received permission to go hunting to provision the mess. He departed with the hopes of all the troops that he would soon return with venison at least.

Not far into the woods, Crockett came upon a freshly killed deer. It had been skinned, and the meat was still warm. He surmised that the Indians responsible were not far away, possibly watching him. Though he despised taking another hunter's kill, he decided that his men needed the meat. He threw the carcass across his horse and rode into camp to a hearty welcome. He was generous with the meat, saving only a small portion for himself.

It is interesting to note the extent to which Crockett elaborated on this event in his 1834 autobiography. Undoubtedly because he was planning a campaign for the presidency, he took the opportunity to extol the virtues of his actions: "I could have sold it for almost any price I would have asked, but this wasn't my rule, neither in peace nor war. Whenever I had anything, and saw a fellow-being suffering, I was more anxious to relieve him than to benefit myself. And this is one of the true secrets of me being a poor man to this day. . . . Yet it has never left my heart empty of consolations which money couldn't buy, the consolation of having sometimes fed the hungry and covered the naked."

The next day, after the army made camp, Crockett went hunting again. He came upon a "large gang of hogs," he wrote. He killed one and scattered the others, which ran toward camp. Crockett soon heard guns firing and hogs squealing. When he arrived back at the camp, he found that the men had slaughtered several hogs, along with a cow that had wandered out of the brush. Though the men ate well that night, they later discovered that they had devoured the livestock of a village of friendly Cherokees in the area. Colonel Coffee gave those Cherokees a receipt from the United States Army for the provisions they had unknowingly provided. Whether or not they ever received compensation is unknown.

The army marched on, returning to Ditto's Landing and then proceeding to Camp Wills near what is now Gadsden and a reunion with Jackson's troops.

After the Creek War ended and Crockett remarried (see the section on Maxwell, Tennessee, pages 41-46), he rode off in the fall of 1816 to explore the Black Warrior Valley for sites where he might move his family. He had seen and liked the land during the war, and he knew that others were moving there. Indeed, the area around what is now Birmingham was settled rather quickly after the Creek War. This was facilitated by the Tennessee soldiers' construction of a wagon road into the upper Black Warrior basin. A man known as Devil John Jones was one of the early settlers in the area. Crockett mentioned passing through Devil John's namesake Jones Valley, which extends southwest from what is now Birmingham along the I-20/I-59 corridor through Bessemer and toward Tuscaloosa. It lies between Rock Mountain and Red Mountain.

Crockett rode with three neighbors named Rich, Robinson, and Frazier from the Bean's Creek settlement. They crossed the Tennessee River at Ditto's Landing and followed the Black Warrior Valley downstream toward the site of Black Warrior Town, which Crockett had helped burn three years earlier. Early in the trip, they stopped for a day to visit an old acquaintance of Crockett's. During that visit, Frazier went hunting and was bitten by a poisonous snake. Crockett, Rich, and Robinson left him in the care of the family and continued on their scouting expedition.

The party continued southwest through Jones Valley and eventually came to a site that Crockett identified as Tuscaloosa (not as Black Warrior Town). The three men camped in the uninhabited area. Though they had hobbled and belled their horses, they heard the animals heading away from them two hours before dawn. When dawn came, Crockett set out on foot to find them, though they had a two-hour head start. Carrying a heavy rifle, he "went ahead the whole day, wading creeks and swamps, and climbing mountains," as he later wrote. He never was able to catch the horses, though people in the cabins he passed along the way all reported having heard their bells as they passed. By the end of the day, Crockett had covered 50 miles on foot, by his own estimate. Exhausted, he returned to the last cabin he had passed and took lodging for the night.

The next morning, he started back south to rejoin his party. About midday, he was overcome with fatigue, fever, and headache and lay down along the path to rest. Soon, a party of Indians came along and offered him some ripe melon, but Crockett was too ill to eat or drink. "They then signed to me," wrote Crockett, "that I would die, and be buried; a thing I was confoundly afraid of myself." By sign, they told him of a cabin a mile and a half away. "I got up to go," Crockett wrote, "but when I rose, I reeled about like a cow with the blind staggers, or a fellow who had taken too many 'horns.' " One of the Indians then took Crockett to the nearby cabin, where he was tended by a woman who served him warm tea.

The next day, two of Crockett's neighbors from home passed through the community. Hearing of his illness, they came to see him and bought him a horse. Since they were going south as Crockett intended to do, they rode with him until he reached his original party of Rich and Robinson. Crockett got worse, not better. He could not even sit up. "I thought," wrote Crockett, "now the jig was mighty nigh up with me."

Rich and Robinson took him to the cabin of the Jesse Jones family. They then bought horses and set off for home, leaving Crockett in the care of strangers. The family tended him for two weeks, during which time he appeared to be near death several times. "And so the woman, who had a bottle of Bateman's drops, thought if they killed me, I would only die any how, and so she would try it with me," Crockett wrote. Fortunately, his fever broke, and he began to feel better after a few days.

A passing wagoner who was heading north to the area near Crockett's Tennessee home agreed to take him along. When they reached the area, Crockett borrowed a horse and rode the last 20 miles to Bean's Creek. "I was so pale and so much reduced," recalled Crockett, "that my face looked like it had been half soled with brown paper." His wife, Elizabeth, was startled to see him. She had been told he was dead. Rich and Robinson had found Crockett's horse along with their own. Perhaps embarrassed to admit they had left him ill and alone, they had declared that Crockett was dead and that they had talked to men who had seen him buried. "I know'd this was a whapper of a lie, as soon as I heard it," Crockett later wrote. (For more information, see the section on Maxwell, Tennessee, pages 41-46.)

Replica sections of the fort's wall are used by reenactors at the site of the massacre. A path marks the outline of Fort Mims.

Fort Mims

The five-acre site of Fort Mims (or Mimms) is located near Tensaw in Baldwin County in southern Alabama. To reach it, take Exit 34 off I-65 and drive north on AL 59. It is four miles to Stockton, then another 11 miles to Boatyard Road (CR 80). Turn west on Boatyard Road and drive three miles to Fort Mims Road, where you'll see a historic marker. The site of Fort Mims is a half-mile north of the marker.

The massacre at Fort Mims on August 30, 1813, ignited the American response that became the Creek War. David Crockett left his home in Tennessee to participate. As a volunteer militia-man, he camped at the site of the massacre 15 months afterward.

The Creek War began as a civil war between two factions of

Creeks. The Shawnee leader Tecumseh came to the Muskogee people (the Creeks) in 1811 at Tookabatcha, south of Tallassee, to rally them in a pan-Indian response against continued western movement by white settlers. The Chickasaws and Choctaws had already refused to join him. The northern Creek villages had fought against the Patriots during the American Revolution, while the southern villages had remained neutral. Despite agreements by Creeks with George Washington and the United States government, settlers in Georgia continued moving west into Creek lands. The Creeks were split in their willingness to join Tecumseh's call for a general uprising. By this time, many Creeks were of mixed blood—some were fathered by Scottish traders—and had ties with two cultures. Those who wanted to wage war on the encroaching settlers carried painted war clubs, which earned them the name Red Sticks. They were led by Peter McQueen and Red Eagle, also known as William Weatherford. Not only did these warring Upper Creeks attack settlers, they threatened the Lower Creeks who either refused to join them or actually fought for the Americans under Creek leaders such as William McIntosh. This faction was known as the White Sticks. They went into battle wearing on their heads a white feather and a deer tail.

In May 1812, a party of five Creek warriors led by Little Warrior was returning home after having followed Tecumseh to his home in the Northwest Territory, where they had agreed to join his pan-Indian uprising. As they passed through the Duck River area of Humphreys County, Tennessee, they attacked a family of women and children. The Creeks murdered the children, left for dead one mother, and took Martha Crawley as a prisoner. Reports of this incident enraged settlers all across Tennessee. Mrs. Crawley escaped in June and hid in the swamps for three days until she was taken in by blacksmith Tandy Walker at Black Warrior Town. Though she was safe, her escape was not known to the Tennesseans. Her kidnapping was used by politicians and the newspapers to fan the flames of hatred of Indians across Tennessee. The truth was bad enough, but the wild exaggerations of her mistreatment by the Red Sticks and the generally accepted notion that the British were behind these Indian atrocities served to assure that the frontier settlers would aggressively fight against the Creeks as part of the War of 1812.

After the Creeks later surrendered to Andrew Jackson, some Red Sticks retreated to Florida, where they fought alongside their Creek cousins, the Seminoles.

The massacre at Fort Mims came in retaliation for an attack by a band of frontier militia on a party of Tallese, Autauga, and Alabama Indians under the leadership of the brutal Peter McQueen. Returning home from Pensacola, this party of warriors was leading a train of packhorses suspected to be laden with ammunition and war supplies, which the settlers feared would be used against them. Indeed, the British, in their prosecution of the War of 1812, were supplying armaments to belligerent tribes and encouraging them to rid the territory of American settlers. Because the American command would send neither regular nor volunteer troops to the area despite repeated petitions, the local settlers mustered a militia to protect themselves. Under the command of Colonel James Caller, 180 militiamen rode east from the Tombigbee and Tensaw area. They intercepted the party of 90 warriors resting at their noonday stop on a pine barren near Burnt Corn Creek. The Battle of Burnt Corn Creek was the start of the Creek War. Thereafter, conflicts between native tribes and settlers escalated dramatically.

Fearing retaliation for the attack at Burnt Corn Creek, the settlers in the Tensaw area, many of mixed Creek heritage, converged on the cabin of Samuel Mims, probably a Creek himself.

Mims had the only loom in the Tensaw region and had constructed a large building to house it. He used the wool produced by area settlers to make his cloth, which he shipped to Mobile. In 1813, cotton was also on the rise as a cash crop in the region.

The anxious settlers built a stockade encompassing a full acre, where they gathered for protection. Soldiers were finally sent to safeguard them. The 265 soldiers garrisoned at Fort Mims were part of the Mississippi volunteers, from the Natchez area. They accounted for nearly half of the 553 souls who took refuge inside the stockade. Not everyone believed the danger was real or imminent. Unfortunately, by some accounts, Major Daniel Beasley, who was in command of the soldiers, was inexplicably unconcerned about fortifying the settlement. His disregard for duty would prove deadly.

By some accounts, Red Eagle, as leader of the Creeks, was more concerned about than belligerent toward the settlers. He and most Creeks had not rallied to Tecumseh's earlier call for a unified rise of Indian nations. Moreover, Red Eagle had entreated

A monument at Fort Mims explains the location of key events in the attack.

the Creek warriors not to attack Fort Mims in reprisal for the attack at Burnt Corn Creek, as members of his extended family had taken shelter there. However, he did not prevail in his argument. Knowing that only an attack against the fort would satisfy those among his people who wanted revenge, Red Eagle agreed reluctantly to lead the war party. He expected that the fort would successfully repel his warriors and that the symbolic gesture of retribution would satisfy them. A party of 1,000 warriors prepared to attack Fort Mims.

Despite Major Beasley's official reports that he had fortified the stockade and was prepared to protect the settlers, he apparently ignored the concerns of his superiors and showed no anxiety about a pending attack. At noon on August 30, 1813, he was playing cards while some of his soldiers danced with young girls inside the stockade. The gates were open and unguarded. No soldiers were posted there as lookouts. This lax posture continued even after an enslaved youth reported that he had seen Indians near the fort. The boy was whipped for telling lies.

Red Eagle was shocked to find these conditions when he arrived at the edge of the clearing. By contrast, his warriors were elated. The warriors had scouted the fort and knew that the east gate was the point at which to attack. The Creeks charged the open east gate from the woods that had hidden their approach. In full force, they yelled their war cries as they ran across the open field. Some accounts say that upon hearing the onrush of warriors, Beasley jumped up and ran to the east gate. He reportedly tried to close the gate himself, but sand had washed into the entrance, so he was unable to move it. He was the first to die as the warriors poured through the gate and into the stockaded settlement, where the 550 inhabitants were taken completely by surprise.

Some historians have challenged that the gate was blocked by sand, though most agree that Beasley was the first to die, facing the attack and giving orders with his last breath. According to other accounts, the Creeks rushed the walls and jammed large branches or poles into the waist-high loopholes through which the settlers inside were supposed to fire their rifles from a kneeling position. The warriors also jammed their own guns through the loopholes from the outside and fired into the fort. With the holes plugged from the outside, the Creeks began to chop at the palisades, ultimately hacking a hole in the stockade's wall. It was through that opening that the onslaught of Red Stick warriors poured. The poor design in placing the loopholes low to the ground is regarded by many historians as the single factor most responsible for the defeat at Fort Mims.

The ensuing massacre was horrific. The warriors slaughtered the settlers and mutilated their bodies until they were unrecognizable. People had huddled in cabins and in the watchtower bastion at the southwest corner of the fort. Throughout the afternoon, they were hunted down in their hiding places, pulled out, and murdered. The warriors retreated after a couple of hours but then returned to burn the fort. The bodies were burned as well. Only three or four dozen settlers survived. A few escaped into the woods through a passage Dr. Thomas Holmes chopped through the fort's wall from inside a cabin during the lull after the massacre. He knew the attackers would return to scalp the dead. Some who used the passage were captured in the forest surrounding the fort and killed, but others made good their escape. Some of the survivors were enslaved Africans, who were taken prisoner by the Creeks. Half the dead were soldiers. The other half were civilian settlers, including about 100 children.

The recently completed watchtower did not burn; it was the only part of the fort to remain intact. It was filled, however, with the bodies of those killed while trying to hide. Unbeknownst to the attackers, a storehouse of arms and powder was beneath the watchtower, protected from discovery by the pile of victims.

This was the attack that enraged the settlers on the frontier in Middle Tennessee, the massacre that caused 2,000 men to leave their homes and enlist in the militia. David Crockett was one of them (see the section on Winchester, Tennessee, pages 38-40).

After serving 90 days under General John Coffee in the first months of the Creek War, Crockett returned home to Bean's Creek in late December 1813 (see the section on Ohatchee, pages 100-105). As the war progressed during 1814, the Red Sticks retreated south and east toward Pensacola. In fact, the Spanish had allowed the British to land there with 300 troops and to train and outfit the Creeks for attacks on Mobile and then New Orleans. To combat this effort, another call went out for volunteers. In September 1814, Crockett enlisted for a six-month tour, to last from September 28 until March 27, 1815. He served as a third sergeant under Major William Russell in the Separate Battalion of Tennessee Mounted Gunmen.

Mustered at Fayetteville, the company of 130 men rode south and crossed the Tennessee River at Muscle Shoals at Melton Bluff. The men followed the Black Warrior River south to the Tombigbee River, then reached the Alabama Cutoff not far from the site of Fort Mims, a couple dozen miles north of Mobile.

Upon arriving in late October or early November, they learned that Andrew Jackson's army had moved east two days earlier. Jackson was headed to Pensacola because he had taken it upon himself to stop the use of the Spanish port to provision the British army and navy for probable attacks on Americans at Mobile and New Orleans. Jackson's army was on foot because the men suspected there was nothing for the horses to eat on the way east. Crockett's company left its horses at the cutoff as well and followed Jackson on foot. "It was about 80 miles off," wrote Crockett, "but in good heart we shouldered our guns, blankets, and provisions, and trudged merrily on."

On November 7, 1814, while Crockett and his fellow militiamen were trying to catch up with the general, Jackson's forces attacked Pensacola. The British, not wanting to fight for the town, called a truce long enough to blow up their powder stored at Fort Barrancas and then to board their ships, which left the town undefended. On November 8, Crockett's company arrived on its trek from the Alabama Cutoff.

Crockett and his men had missed all the action. "That evening we went down into the town," wrote Crockett, "and could see the British fleet lying in sight of the place. We got some liquor, and took a 'horn' or so, and went back to the camp." The next day, Crockett and his companions joined all of Jackson's troops in marching back west toward the cutoff. They reached the site of Fort Mims and made camp.

After resting at Fort Mims awhile, Jackson's forces marched west to Mobile, then to New Orleans. Crockett and his company marched a mile and a half from the ruins of Fort Mims to Fort Montgomery, where they remained a few days provisioning themselves by slaughtering the cattle, which had become wild after the settlers' massacre some 15 months earlier. The company then headed east again toward Florida, looking for Red Stick warriors (see the next section on Pensacola, Florida).

Historic Pensacola Village includes houses David
Crockett might have seen during his Creek War
campaign of 1814.

FLORIDA

Pensacola

*Pensacola is in the extreme west end of the Florida Pan
handle at the intersection of I-10 and US 29. Historic Pensacola
Village, administered by West Florida University, interprets the
history of the city through displays housed in several buildings in the Seville Historic District. Two of the homes date to
1804 and 1805. The village includes several blocks centered
around Zaragoza (or Zarragossa) Street and Tarragona Street.
The visitor center is at 205 East Zaragoza Street. The Historic Pensacola Museum, operated by the Pensacola Historical
Society, offers displays interpreting several periods of Pensacola
history. The museum is located at 115 East Zaragoza.*

David Crockett made two separate excursions to Pensacola in
the fall of 1814. These two military campaigns were made within a
few days of each other.

After marching 80 miles from the Alabama Cutoff, Crockett and his fellow volunteers arrived late to the surrender of Pensacola by the British on November 8, 1814. Before abandoning the town and retreating to their ships, the British destroyed the powder they had stored at Fort Barrancas. That fort is now part of a National Park Service site on the Pensacola Naval Air Station. It is open to the public, but access requires a security check at the air station's gate.

Seeing that the British had abandoned town, Crockett and his companions went into town and had a few drinks—which he called taking "a horn." The next day, the men began the 80-mile march back toward the Alabama Cutoff.

After camping near the ruins of Fort Mims for a few days, the command of which Crockett was a part returned to the Pensacola area to search for parties of hostile Red Sticks. Under the general command of Major Uriah Blue of Virginia, Crockett and the rest of his company under Major William Russell left Fort Montgomery in late November 1814 to search north and east of Pensacola all the way to the Apalachicola River. Among the 1,000 men were some 180 Chickasaw and Choctaw warriors. Eventually, the large party made its way to the area just north of Pensacola. As the men camped along the Escambia River, a boat arrived from Pensacola bringing supplies such as coffee, sugar, and liquor. If you care to see the river much as Crockett witnessed it, you can cross it within the Escambia River Water Management District, located about 12 miles north of I-10 along US 29, then six miles east along FL 184.

The Chickasaws and Choctaws convinced the major to let them cross the river. Crockett and 15 other men from Russell's company went with them. Soon, they came to a flooded area. "The whole country was covered with water, and looked like a sea," Crockett later wrote. "We didn't stop for this, though, but just put in like so many spaniels, and waded on, sometimes up to our armpits." The men covered a mile and a half in this fashion before they emerged and built a fire to warm and dry themselves.

After proceeding about six miles upstream, two of the Indian scouts returned with news of a Creek camp nearby. They wanted to attack and kill the inhabitants, so they prepared for battle by painting their faces and bodies. They also painted Major Russell because he was their leader.

Before the men could reach the Creek camp—which they soon discovered was on an island and inaccessible—they heard shots and a war whoop nearby. Running in that direction, Crockett and his party found that two of their scouts had come upon a pair of Creeks, whom they had tricked and killed. The scouts had beheaded the enemy warriors and were hitting the severed heads with clubs in a victory ritual. They handed a club to Crockett, who joined in. He later related that the Chickasaws and Choctaws then gathered around him, slapped him on the shoulder, and declared, "Warrior, warrior." The victors then scalped the severed heads.

Crockett, his fellow soldiers, and the Chickasaw and Choctaw warriors headed back toward the Escambia River—or the "Scamby,"

Crockett waded through the flood plain of the "Scamby" River in the late fall of 1814.

as Crockett called it—where they came across a family of Spaniards who had been killed and scalped. "I began to feel mighty ticklish along about this time, for I know'd if there was no danger then, there had been, and I felt exactly like there still was," Crockett wrote.

Moving downriver, they soon arrived opposite the Creek camp on the island. Some of the Chickasaw and Choctaw warriors hailed the camp and spoke across the river to a woman, who told them that the camp's canoe was on their side. It had been taken across by two men of the camp who were looking for their horses, she said. "They were the same two we had killed," Crockett wrote. Forty raiders crossed by turns in the canoe and took the unsuspecting camp, capturing the women and children but noting that the warriors had all escaped.

Major Russell directed his company to proceed up the Escambia to where it became the Conecuh River, which Crockett called the "Conaker." Before the two Creeks were murdered, Russell's scouts had learned from them that a town sat farther up the river with "cattle and plenty to eat," according to Crockett. The troops were running low on rations. As Russell's forces moved upstream, Crockett was sent by canoe with two others to paddle by moonlight to Major Blue's camp for provisions. Upon arriving, they learned that Blue wanted Russell to return, which he did promptly after one of Crockett's company traveled upstream by sunrise with the orders.

The reunited force marched south and crossed the Escambia River at Miller's Landing. Two companies subsequently pursued some Creeks along the east side of Pensacola Bay. It is unclear if Crockett was with them. In any event, some prisoners were taken. As they were being marched back to Fort Montgomery, they were killed and scalped by their Indian escorts.

From the camp where Crockett had arrived by canoe, the combined military force marched east toward the Apalachicola River. Clearing this area of hostile Creeks and Seminoles had been their original orders when they left Fort Montgomery 34 days earlier. They had subsisted during that time on 20 days' worth of flour rations and eight days' worth of beef rations. Crockett recounted, "We were, therefore, in extreme suffering for want of something to eat, and exhausted with our exposure and the fatigues of our journey. I remember well, that I had not myself tasted bread but twice in nineteen days." He claimed that he and his companions had survived to that point on coffee.

That December, Major Russell's men advanced east from the Escambia and Conecuh rivers looking for renegade Creeks. Scouts reported a Creek village along what Crockett called the "Chatahachy" (Chattahoochee) River. The soldiers advanced eagerly, anticipating a hearty meal after taking Holm's Village. "We made a furious charge on the town," wrote Crockett, "but to our great mortification and surprise, there was not a human being in it." Finding no provisions, as the inhabitants had carried everything off with them, the army burned the town. Crockett and his fellow soldiers returned to their camp "as nearly starved as any set of poor fellows ever were in the world," he wrote.

Having arrived at the Apalachicola River as ordered, Major Blue's force was divided. One part marched west toward Baton Rouge in an attempt to join General Andrew Jackson on his campaign to New Orleans. Crockett and the rest of Major Russell's company marched northwest toward Fort Decatur on the Tallapoosa River with the intention of returning to Fort Strother (see the section on Sylacauga, Alabama, pages 112-15).

Pleasant Gardens was home to Congressman Sam Carson, a friend of David Crockett.

NORTH CAROLINA

Pleasant Gardens

Pleasant Gardens is a small McDowell County community located on US 70 west of Marion and east of Old Fort. It is also the name of two noted local homes, one formerly belonging to the Joseph McDowell family and the other to the Carson family. The Historic Carson House sits along US 70 some 1.5 miles west of NC 226 and along Buck Creek just above its confluence with the Catawba River.

The Historic Carson House proudly boasts, "Davy Crockett Slept Here," which comes as a surprise to visitors who are unfamiliar with Crockett's North Carolina connections.

David Crockett occasionally stopped at the home of Samuel Carson and the Carson family while he was in North Carolina visiting his wife's family, the Pattons, in Swannanoa. This was his probable destination when he created David Crockett's Bridle Trail (see the section on Fairview, pages 140-42). It was also the home to which he rode in haste in 1827 to report to the family the outcome of the Vance-Carson duel (see the section on Tuxedo, pages 142-48).

Construction of the original home was begun in 1793 by Colonel John Carson. He built a single-pen (or single-room), two-story log cabin over a full cellar. Around 1800, he added a second single-pen, two-story cabin. They were joined by a dogtrot, or open hall. The entrance hall is now that passageway. The dining room occupies one cabin; the living room occupies the other. Additional living space was added over the years. Improvements have masked the underlying structure.

About two miles east of the Carson House sat the home of Joseph McDowell. It was named Pleasant Gardens. John Carson married McDowell's widow in 1797. Mary Moffitt McDowell moved into the Carson House and brought with her the name of her former residence, Pleasant Gardens. In her second home of that name, she gave birth in 1798 to a son, Samuel Price Carson.

Besides serving as a North Carolina legislator, Samuel Carson was elected to the United States Congress in 1825 at age 26. He was reelected in 1827 in a bitter campaign that resulted in his duel with Dr. Robert Vance. Carson was a strong supporter of Andrew Jackson. He served in Congress alongside Sam Houston and Crockett, though Carson's friendship with Crockett was strained for a time by Crockett's antagonism toward President Jackson.

An extraordinarily handsome young man, Carson was often seen in the company of Jackson's niece, Emily Donelson, who frequently acted as hostess at the White House after the death of Rachel Jackson just before the president was inaugurated. As did Crockett, however, Carson eventually broke from his support of Jackson.

For political, personal, and health reasons, Sam Carson departed North Carolina for Texas in 1835. He purchased 3,000 acres in the Red River Valley at Pecan Point near the Texas-Arkansas border. In February 1836, he was elected by his fellow Texans to represent them at the Constitutional Convention in March. This was the same convention Crockett may have hoped to attend as an elected representative (see the section on San Augustine, Texas, pages 209-10). At the convention in Washington, Texas, Carson was almost elected the interim president of Texas. Instead, he was elected the first secretary of state. About this time in the formation of the Republic of Texas, Carson and the other delegates heard that the Alamo had fallen. Carson learned that his friend David Crockett was among the dead.

Swannanoa

Swannanoa lies along the Swannanoa River and I-40 near the town of Black Mountain about eight miles east of Asheville. Those interested in the life of David Crockett will find several sites of interest in the region.

The Swannanoa Valley Museum in Black Mountain interprets the history of the valley by means of a scale relief map and numerous displays about the various phases of the area's history. A photo on display shows the Elizabeth Patton Crockett grave monument in Acton, Texas. The museum is two blocks west on US 70 from NC 9.

The Robert Patton homesite is five miles west of Black Mountain. To reach it, take Exit 59 off I-40. Patton Cove Road leads north for 0.4 mile to US 70. Turn left (west) on US 70, go 0.3 mile, turn right (north) on Riverwood Road, drive half a mile to

Bee Tree Road, turn right, go 0.2 mile to Patton Cemetery Road, turn left (north), and proceed uphill for half a mile to the Patton Cemetery, on the left. Here were made the earliest burials of non-native people in southwest North Carolina. The Robert Patton Meeting House was located adjacent to the west side of the Patton Cemetery. A Presbyterian church erected in the 1780s and used until 1839, it was the principal gathering place for community meetings during the early settlement of the Swannanoa Valley. The site of the old meeting house is on private property. Nothing remains of the structure today. The Robert Patton home sat along an old wagon road that ran parallel to the north side of Bee Tree Road. A private residence now occupies that spot at the corner of Patton Cemetery Road and Bee Tree Road adjacent to W. D. Williams Elementary School.

Return to Bee Tree Road and turn right (northwest). Within a half-mile is Swannanoa Presbyterian Church (or Piney Grove Church), which replaced the function of the Robert Patton Meeting House in 1839. Continue on Bee Tree Road, then bear left at Warren Wilson Road, which circles the campus of Warren Wilson College and returns to US 70 after a four-mile loop. The land encircled by this route and lying on both sides of the Swannanoa River was part of the 1,000 acres where Robert Patton, the father-in-law of David Crockett, lived. Though nothing remains of the Patton homestead, a cabin from his plantation that was used by slaves was moved in 1961 to the Vance Birthplace State Historic Site northeast of Asheville on Reems Creek Road. To see it, take Exit 21 (New Stock Road) off US 23/US 19 at Weaverville and proceed six miles to the state historic site.

The Swannanoa Valley was the home of Robert Patton, father of Elizabeth Patton, the second wife of David Crockett. Patton was a large landowner in the highlands above the Catawba River in what was at one time Burke County. Crockett visited this home on several occasions and was well known in Swannanoa and the surrounding area.

By his own account, Crockett did well in his second marriage, which came in 1816. Elizabeth was "a good industrious woman," wrote Crockett, "and owned a snug little farm [in Tennessee] and lived quite comfortable." She had Patton as both her maiden name and her married name from her first marriage. She had married her first cousin James, the son of Elijah Patton, a brother to Robert.

Crockett visited the Patton home in the Swannanoa Valley on several occasions during their marriage. One story tells that a large oak called "the Target Tree" stood in front of the home. Robert Patton and Crockett, his marksman son-in-law, reportedly held shooting matches there.

One writer claimed that Crockett pursued Elizabeth all the

A slave cabin from the Patton plantation sits at Vance Birthplace State Historic Site.

way to Swannanoa to propose marriage to her in 1816, noting that she had returned to North Carolina after her husband died. That same writer related that Crockett had fought alongside James Patton in the Creek War and had returned James's personal possessions to Elizabeth to fulfill his dying request. This notion is highly suspect. Most historians concur that David and Elizabeth married in Bean's Creek, Tennessee, where he pursued her as a suitor.

After his election to the United States Congress in 1827, Crockett and his family traveled to Swannanoa from their West Tennessee home. Crockett drove horses to North Carolina. Along the way, he suffered a relapse of his malaria and was ill for a long time at Swannanoa. This delayed his family's return to Tennessee, but it also put Crockett in place to witness one of the most notorious events of the era—the Vance-Carson duel, which took place on November 5 of that year (see the section on Tuxedo, pages 142-48).

A few days after the duel, apparently sufficiently recovered from his relapse of malaria, Crockett made his way to Washington

The Patton Cemetery was adjacent to the Patton Meeting House, built by Robert Patton.

for his first congressional session. Most likely, he rode in a carriage in the company of Congressman Samuel Carson. Given the geographic isolation of western North Carolina at the time, Carson and Crockett traveled west, then north through Tennessee. They probably took the Buncombe Turnpike through Asheville, then followed the French Broad River through Alexander to Painted Rock, where the turnpike joined the Tennessee Road to Greeneville. They then headed northeast to Abingdon, Virginia, and on to Washington. A historic marker in Marshall, North Carolina, which sits along the French Broad River northwest of Asheville, commemorates the Buncombe Turnpike. (For information on Crockett's congressional career, see the section on Washington, District of Columbia, pages 157-69.)

Fairview

Fairview lies on US 74A southeast of Asheville in Buncombe County. What was formerly called David Crockett's Bridle Trail is known today as Old Fort Road. Lying south of the Swannanoa Mountains, it departs US 74A in Fairview some four miles southeast of the US 74A and I-40 interchange (Exit 53) and 1.2 miles south of where US 74A passes through Mine Hole Gap. A granite marker at the Spring Mountain Community Center on Old Fort Road 4.1 miles east of US 74A at Fairview commemorates "Davy Crockett's Bridle Trail."

The exact route Crockett took after reaching what is now NC 9 is unknown, but Crooked Creek Road off TN 9 (located 1.1 miles southeast of Old Fort Road) leads 10 miles along Mount Hebron Road and Bat Cave Road into Old Fort from the south. After passing under I-40, Bat Cave Road becomes

Catawba Avenue and leads 0.4 mile to the Mountain Gateway Museum and another 0.2 mile to the Old Fort Train Depot and Museum. Crockett most likely rode the route where Mount Hebron Road and Bat Cave Road (Catawba Avenue) follow Crooked Creek downstream. Crooked Creek continues downstream to the Catawba River, along which Sam Carson lived at Pleasant Gardens. Crockett was a frequent guest at that home.

Fairview is the beginning point of what was once David Crockett's Bridle Trail.

Around 1816, early in his second marriage, Crockett was visiting his wife's family at the Patton home when he became outraged at what he called "the political shenanigans" that authorized the building of a tollgate on the road on the face of the mountain east of Swannanoa Gap. In protest, Crockett and some other men marked a separate bridle trail so they and others who did not want to pay the toll could get up and down the mountain. For many

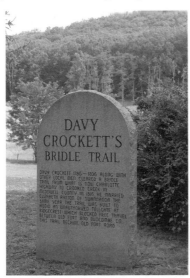

A monument for Davy Crockett's Bridle Trail is on the south side of the Swannanoa Mountains.

years, the route was known to locals as David Crockett's Bridle Trail.

Years later, Crockett's reputation inspired local residents to recount encounters they had in North Carolina with the famous frontiersman. One story told of Crockett and his party stopping by the Mary Canady Whitaker cabin along the bridle trail to get water. Crockett stayed for a meal and then took lodging for the night. Another recounted a hunting incident in which Samuel McBrayer shot a wild turkey and heard another rifle fire as he pulled his own trigger. As both men approached the kill from different angles along the bridle trail, McBrayer discovered that he and David Crockett had simultaneously shot the same bird. They divided the quarry. And 15-year-old Elizabeth Cooper Hill claimed to have played the fiddle while Crockett danced in her home in 1826. Most certainly, Crockett was no stranger to residents of the area.

Tuxedo

Tuxedo lies on US 25 south of Asheville. It is about 10 miles west of I-26. A historic marker sits alongside Old US 25 about 2.5 miles south of Tuxedo in extreme south Henderson County. The incident commemorated took place about a mile south, just over the state line in South Carolina.

The Tuxedo area was the site of one of the most infamous events of the era, the Vance-Carson duel of 1827, to which David Crockett was a witness.

Crockett was first elected to the United States Congress that year. Following his election victory, he took his family with him on a trip from their home in Tennessee to North Carolina to see his wife's family, the Pattons. Along the way, he suffered a relapse of malaria and spent weeks recovering at the Patton home. The illness put him in the area at the time of the duel.

The Vance-Carson duel grew out of a series of events that began in a previous generation. As had Crockett's father, Robert Patton served the Patriot cause during the Revolutionary War. Both men were connected to the events surrounding the Battle of Kings Mountain. However, unlike John Crockett, Robert Patton received a sizable land grant for his service.

In the fall of 1780, British major Patrick Ferguson was advancing into the North Carolina Piedmont as the left flank of General Lord Charles Cornwallis's army attempted to execute its Southern strategy. Advancing from its victory at Camden, this army fed itself by plundering the livestock of Patriot sympathizers. In Burke County, known for its herds of beef cattle, Colonel Charles McDowell saw the need to protect livestock from Ferguson. To do so, he gathered some of the prominent Patriots of the upper Catawba Valley and asked them to participate in a ruse. Robert Patton was

Congressman Sam Carson and Dr. Robert Brank Vance crossed into South Carolina at Saluda Gap for their deadly 1827 duel.

one of the leaders. Under McDowell's proposal, Patton and others were to ride to Gilbert Town and "take protection" under the British in order to preserve their livestock. McDowell told the men that their apparent capitulation to British authority was necessary, and that it was understood their actions were not true expressions of their allegiance.

After listening to the plan, Robert Patton flatly refused to take protection for whatever purpose. Others agreed with his stance. Instead, they drove cattle from the upper Catawba Valley into the high coves of Black Mountain to keep them away from the British army. In 1784, for this and other service to the Patriot cause, Patton was given a claim by General Griffith Rutherford for 1,000 acres of North Carolina land.

Other Burke County leaders saw matters differently and agreed to participate in McDowell's ruse. One of those who took protection was Captain John Carson, later promoted and widely revered as Colonel Carson. His apparent capitulation to the British, though actually an act of patriotism, would haunt his family for decades and lead one of his sons, a friend of David Crockett, into a deadly duel.

The record of John Carson's patriotism is supported by a deception he perpetrated on the advancing army. When the soldiers arrived in Burke County, Carson led them to a substantial herd of cattle. Only after they had slaughtered 100 head did Carson mention that the animals belonged to local Tories. The incident greatly upset the Loyalists in the area, and mention of the egregious error made its way to England. Major Ferguson admitted that he had been outwitted by the Patriots.

Dr. Robert Brank Vance was the son of Colonel David Vance, who had built his home along Reems Creek in the late 1700s. David Vance had fought at Kings Mountain and was an influential man of Burke County, which at the time included what is now Buncombe County. Robert Vance was friends with Samuel Carson of Pleasant Gardens, who had served two terms in the state senate beginning at age 24. Vance became the area's first physician and worked for three years as a doctor until he won $5,000 in a lottery, at which time he retired from medical practice and became interested in politics. In 1825, he ran for a seat in the United States Congress against his friend Carson and lost.

Determined to win the next election, Vance took the counsel of some political advisers. Unfortunately, following their advice, he chose to impugn the reputation and patriotism of his opponent. It was during a campaign debate in 1827 in Morganton that Vance attacked the Carson family. According to published accounts written by Silas McDowell, Vance remarked with vehemence, "The Bible tells us that 'because the fathers have eaten sour grapes, their sons' teeth have been set on edge. . . .' My father never ate sour grapes and my competitor's father did. . . . In the time of the Revolutionary War, my father, Colonel [David] Vance, stood up to the fight, while my competitor's father, Colonel [John] Carson, skulked, and took British protection."

The accusation so outraged the Carson family that the several brothers of Samuel Carson who were attending had to be restrained from rushing the stage to attack Vance.

Vance had previously insulted Carson in Asheville, insinuating that he had taken money from the public till rather than from his own pocket to help with charity. When Carson had rebutted that remark but hadn't challenged Vance to a duel, Vance believed Carson would not fight him at all. Thus, he felt he could continue slandering his former friend with impunity. Carson was mistaken.

John Carson wrote an angry letter to Vance. Vance replied that he could not fight a man of John Carson's age, but that one of

Carson's sons might stand in his place. When pressed on the matter, Vance said, "Sam knows well enough I mean him." Because dueling was illegal in North Carolina, Samuel Carson issued his demand for redress from Jonesborough, Tennessee, through a friend, General Alney Burgin.

The duel was set for three weeks hence. It would take place just over the North Carolina line in South Carolina, near Saluda Gap. The seconds and the physicians for each party were in place. The men would walk 10 paces and, upon the count of "Fire, one, two, three," discharge their weapons. Though it was common on the field of honor for each man to fire his pistol into the air to save life and face, such was not the case here. Warren C. Davis of South Carolina, well schooled in the art and practice of *code duello*, or dueling, would serve as second to Sam Carson. Carson told Davis that he would shoot Vance wherever Vance desired, which meant he intended only to wound him. But Davis was convinced that Vance intended to kill Carson. As the two men gathered for the duel, Davis told Carson he would serve as his second only if Carson promised to shoot Vance with the intent to kill. Reluctantly, Carson agreed.

The men stepped off their paces, turned, and fired. Carson's shot hit Vance in his side. The bullet did not exit. Vance fell to the ground without discharging his weapon. Though he tried to approach Vance to speak to him, Carson was led away by his attendants. The mortally wounded Vance was carried to a nearby hotel—possibly that owned by Warren Davis—where he survived for 32 hours. He remarked to his aides that he held no ill will for Carson and regretted that he had not been allowed to speak to him after the duel.

Crockett, who witnessed the duel but whose role in it is otherwise unknown, jumped on his horse and rode hard for Pleasant

Gardens with the news. Most likely, he followed the Buncombe Turnpike, which had been opened just that year to connect Greenville, South Carolina, with Greeneville, Tennessee, by way of Asheville. He passed through what are now Flat Rock and Hendersonville, probably along a route that became US 25, then rode north across the plateau through what is now Fletcher and then Asheville before crossing the Swannanoa River at the mouth of Sweeten Creek where US 25 and NC 81 (Swannanoa Road) meet today. Along the turnpike, he probably encountered droves of cattle, hogs, mules, and turkeys being driven to market in Charleston, South Carolina, from farms as far away as Kentucky and Tennessee. At the Swannanoa River, he probably turned east and followed David Crockett's Bridle Trail down the mountain (see the section on Fairview, pages 140-42). Samuel Carson's daughter recalled that Crockett rode hurriedly to the Carson home, Pleasant Gardens, waving his hat and shouting, "The victory is ours!"

Unbeknownst to Crockett and perhaps to anyone else except family friend Silas McDowell, Vance may have used the duel to fulfill a death wish. On the day he insulted the Carson family, Vance had remarked to McDowell in a boardinghouse in Morganton that he hoped Carson would fight and perhaps kill him. Vance apparently saw his path to Congress blocked and was despondent over the prospect of returning to his medical practice or taking up some other career. "I do wish for him to kill me," Vance said to McDowell, who recorded the words 50 years later. "Perhaps, it would save me from self-slaughter."

Killing Robert Vance changed Samuel Carson's life. He served six more years in Congress, but after being defeated in 1833, he brooded over the taking of Vance's life. It affected his mood and his health. He said he was haunted by visions of Vance dying. In part to escape from local reminders of the tragedy that had destroyed his peace of mind, Carson moved to Texas in 1835 (see the section on Pleasant Gardens, pages 134-36).

At age 12, David Crockett drove cattle from his father's tavern to a spot near Natural Bridge.

Natural Bridge

Natural Bridge, a National Historic Landmark, is in southeast Rockbridge County in Virginia's Shenandoah Valley at the intersection of US 11 and VA 130. It is accessible from I-81; US 11 departs the interstate both north and south of Natural Bridge. As a youth, David Crockett drove cattle to a site near here.

In general, US 11 follows the route of the Great Philadelphia Wagon Road through the Shenandoah Valley. Another well-traveled route, the Wilderness Road, ran southwest of Big Lick (what is now Roanoke) and extended to Abingdon and Cumberland Gap.

In 1798, when David Crockett was 12, his father hired him out to Jacob Siler, a Dutchman, to help drive a large herd of cattle to

Rockbridge County, Virginia. Young David joined the drive at his home, the Crockett Tavern, located on the Knoxville-Abingdon Road (see the section on Morristown, Tennessee, pages 13-20).

He walked 400 miles on foot, urging the cattle forward and keeping them headed along the road. The drovers stopped at the home of Siler's father-in-law, a man named Hartley, "at the place," Crockett wrote, "which was three miles from what is called the Natural Bridge." Siler, regarded by Crockett as very kind, paid him "five or six dollars" and praised his work. In fact, he invited Crockett to remain with him to work as an indentured servant. Crockett was probably too young and inexperienced to understand the arrangement that was being suggested. An indentured servant agreed by contract with his employer to long-term servitude in return for food, board, and perhaps training, as in the case of an apprentice. Historians agree that Crockett complied with Siler's suggestion, having been so sternly treated by his own father that he dared not challenge what this adult man told him to do.

After a few weeks, Crockett was playing by the road with some other boys when three wagons came along, one driven by a man Crockett knew from his stops at the tavern in Tennessee. The man's name was Dunn. Young Crockett explained his situation and his desire to return home. Dunn agreed to help him if Crockett would meet him in the morning seven miles south at the ordinary (or inn) where the wagoners would spend the night.

Crockett returned to Siler's house and gathered his belongings while the family was out of the house. He went to bed early and lay all night unable to sleep, filled with anticipation at seeing his parents again and fear at being caught in his escape. Three hours before sunrise, he arose quietly and stepped outside to discover that it was snowing heavily. Though he could not see well because of the blowing snow, he made his way a half-mile through the woods to the wagon road, then turned south. The snow fell so rapidly that by dawn his footprints were covered over and pursuit by Siler was thwarted. Crockett pressed on during the next two hours and arrived at the wagoners' lodging with an hour to spare. The men were up and preparing their horses. Young Crockett was welcomed gladly, warmed by the fire, and fed a good breakfast. With that, they began the journey toward his home.

As they made their way along the road, the going was much too slow for a boy eager to see his parents. After they stayed the night on the Roanoke River at the home of a Mr. Cole, Crockett parted from his friends, deciding he could travel faster on foot. Fortunately for him, he soon met a man who had an extra horse he let Crockett ride. They rode together until they arrived within 15 miles of the Crockett Tavern, where they parted company. Crockett walked south toward home, while the "kind gentleman," as Crockett regarded him, took the road to Kentucky. (For more information, see the section on Morristown, Tennessee, pages 13-20.)

Radford

The Wilderness Road crossed the New River about one mile north of where the I-81 bridge stands near Radford in Montgomery County today. The river is accessible from Radford Riverview Park some 1.5 miles north of I-81 on VA 232 at Exit 105. Turn left at Cowan Street to reach the park. The site where the Wilderness Road crossed the river is on private property that previously hosted an outdoor drama about local frontier heroine Mary Draper Ingles, who was captured by Shawnees near Blacksburg in 1755 and taken to Ohio. She later escaped and crossed hundreds of miles of wilderness to return home.

The Wilderness Road Regional Museum is in nearby Newbern at 5240 Wilderness Road. Take the Dublin exit (Exit 98) off I-81 and follow the brown signs along VA 611, which continues east to the New River and in places follows the historic Wilderness Road.

A marker in Fort Chiswell commemorates the Wilderness Road. It stands along the north-side frontage road at Milepost 81 on I-81, some 24 miles south of Radford. The frontage road is accessible from Exit 80 (US 52) at Fort Chiswell.

At age 13, David Crockett ran away from his Tennessee home. He had been skipping school and hiding his truancy from his father. When his father, who had been drinking, found out, he chased Crockett on foot in a rage. The young Crockett escaped by hiding in the brush. Knowing he couldn't return home for a while, he hired himself out as a drover. His three-year adventure took him as far as Baltimore. Around 1801 (Crockett's account is indefinite), he decided to walk back home. He had worked for several months awaiting a promised ride south with a wagoner named Adam Myers, who had cheated him out of what money he had earned. With three dollars in his pocket—money given him by a group of wagoners he befriended along the road—he set out for home.

According to Crockett's account, this small sum of money supported him as far as the courthouse in Montgomery County at Christiansburg, where he had to stop and work. He labored for a month for James Caldwell, which earned him five dollars, then hired himself out on a four-year contract as an indentured servant to a hatter named Elijah Griffith. Whether he hoped to learn the trade or simply worked as a laborer is unknown. After Crockett

The historic route of the Wilderness Road, used by David Crockett, is commemorated at several places in southwest Virginia, including Fort Chiswell.

worked 18 months, the hatter found himself in debt and departed without paying Crockett. Following that sad turn of events, Crockett found what work he could over the next few weeks and saved enough to buy some clothes.

With new clothes and new determination, Crockett set off from Montgomery County. He followed the Wilderness Road southwest to the New River near what is now Radford. He hoped to find a ferryman to take him across, but the day was cold and the river high, fast, and rough. "The whitecaps were flying," he wrote years later. No one would agree to take Crockett across under those conditions. However, seeing his determination, someone relented and let him take a canoe across on his own. This remedy to his problem was entirely Crockett's idea, for he was eager to get home at last.

He tied his bundle of clothes into the canoe and pushed off into the river. Almost immediately, he regretted his decision. A cold wind was blowing, and the water was quite choppy. He turned the canoe into the current and paddled hard upstream. The current carried him across after he had paddled what he judged to be two miles. "When I struck land," he said, "my canoe was about half full of water, and I was as wet as a drowned rat." His clothes frozen to his body, he had to walk three miles to find a cabin where he could warm himself. When he arrived there, he took what was offered, a drink of spirits. He called it "a leetle of the creater" and declared that it made him "feel so good."

After warming himself inside and out, Crockett continued his trip home. After many miles, he crossed into Tennessee and found his brother John at his home in Sullivan County. (Though Crockett in his autobiography did not identify the brother as John, other writers have said it was he.) John had joined Crockett on the drove when Crockett ran away from home. Crockett stayed with him for a few weeks before resuming the walk to their father's home. He had been gone for three years. He was unsure of the reception he would get but felt compelled to return by his desire to see his family (see the section on Morristown, Tennessee, pages 13-20).

The Gerard House was almost 60 years old at the time Crockett plowed the nearby fields in 1800 after running away from home.

Gerrardstown

Gerrardstown is on WV 51 at Mill Creek about three miles west of I-81, five miles north of the Virginia-West Virginia line. A historic marker on WV 51 commemorates the town settled in 1743 but not officially founded until 1787 by the Reverend David Gerard of Mill Creek Baptist Church. The Gerard House (yes, only one r), built in 1743 by John Hays, is on Congress Street 100 yards west of WV 51. This house was over 50 years old when David Crockett was in the community working as a boy.

The historic National Road (or National Pike) extended from Hagerstown, Maryland, to Frederick and then toward Baltimore. It was most likely the route Crockett and Adam

At age 13, David Crockett ran away from home in fear of his father and embarked on a three-year adventure that took him as far as Baltimore. Gerrardstown was then a Virginia town in the Opequon River Valley that Crockett described as being "below" Winchester. By that, he meant it was downstream and toward the Potomac River. He stayed and worked here in the fall of 1799 and the winter of 1799-1800 while Adam Myers, a wagoner who had offered him a ride back to Tennessee, looked for a load to take south. (For more information, see the section on Cheek's Cross-roads, Tennessee, pages 10-13.)

The Pennsylvania Avenue site of Mrs. Ball's Boarding House, where Crockett lived while in Washington, is occupied today by the Federal Trade Commission.

Washington

The nation's capital in the District of Columbia was known as Washington City in the early 19th century. David Crockett served as a congressman in the Capitol.

Mrs. Ball's Boarding House, where Crockett frequently lodged during his service in Congress, was located on Pennsylvania Avenue between Sixth and Seventh streets. It may have moved to new quarters but stayed on that block. The Federal Trade Commission now occupies the site of one known address for the boardinghouse.

David Crockett arrived in Washington in time for the opening of his first congressional session on December 3, 1827. Though unfamiliar with politics on the national stage, he learned quickly. As a congressman from Tennessee, he considered himself a "Jackson man," a champion of the beliefs of the presidential candidate who had won the popular vote in 1824 but had been defeated by John Quincy Adams when the vote was thrown into the House of Representatives. Unfortunately, Crockett soon found that the business of the nation operated at its own pace. He wrote to a friend, "Thare is no chance of hurrying bussiness here like in the legislature of a State thare is Such a deposition here to Show Eloquence that this will be a long Session and do no good."

Crockett almost immediately introduced legislation known as the Tennessee Vacant Land Bill. This bill would consume his energy for the remainder of his service in Congress. He wanted the federal government to relinquish its claim on certain lands in Tennessee to the state so it could be sold to support education. Crockett assumed the state would sell the land at a low-enough price that the poor—who were the majority of his constituents—could afford it. The complication that would thwart him for the next several years was that the state planned to sell the land at high prices. In response, Crockett, a former state representative, proposed that the federal government sell the land directly to the squatters and bypass the state of Tennessee. In proposing this, he wrote glowingly of his constituents as "hardy sons of the soil; men who had entered the country when it lay in cane, and opened in the wilderness a home for their wives and children."

During the two legislative sessions of the 20th Congress, Crockett worked doggedly but ineffectively on his land bill. In the process, he alienated many who might have been his political allies, including the other representatives from Tennessee, some of the North Carolina delegation, including his friend Sam Carson, and the Jacksonians. By the end of his first term, he had no land-bill victory to take to the electorate. Nonetheless, he did win reelection for a second term.

Crockett supported the expenditure of federal funds for internal improvements to roads and navigable waterways. Representatives from the East saw these expenditures as unnecessary mainly because their areas already had transportation adequate to enhance their commerce. Those in the West needed improvements to encourage economic growth in their areas.

Andrew Jackson, elected president in 1828, saw internal improvements as pork-barrel politics and was against them. This stance aggravated Crockett and was part of the reason he broke with Jackson. Whereas Jackson had wanted military roads built when he was a soldier, he now vetoed legislation to construct roads for commerce. This led Crockett to declare that he was "still a Jackson man but General Jackson is not."

In February 1830, a bill was introduced before Congress autho rizing the removal of Indians from lands east of the Mississippi. Crockett had an interesting history of responses to this cause. Many claim that he was a friend of the native people and that he championed their remaining on their land in direct opposition to the bill, which Jackson supported. The evidence of Crockett's support that is often cited is a speech officially recorded in the *Register of Debates in Congress*. In its printed form, it was titled "A Sketch of the Remarks of the Hon. David Crockett, Representative from Tennessee, on the Bill for the Removal of the Indians, Made in the House of Representatives, Wednesday, May 19, 1830." Unfortunately, biographer James Shackford claimed that Crockett never delivered that speech and did not even write it. Shackford proposed convincingly that Crockett had formed an alliance with Eastern interests to support his land bill. Those New Englanders were opposed to the Indian Removal Bill and required Crockett's support. Crockett's constituents, however, were in favor of the bill and eagerly sought the land the Indians would vacate. Those poor Western constituents, however, were not likely to happen upon the *Debates*. Moreover, many have inferred from Crockett's autobiography that he had not changed his view of Indians. His claim that "we shot them like dogs," written in 1833 in reference to the 1813 slaughter at Tallasehatchee, certainly did not suggest a change of heart (see the section on Tallasehatchee, Alabama, pages 105-9).

Nevertheless, Crockett declared in his autobiography that he voted against Jackson's "infamous Indian bill," which he called a "wicked, unjust measure." He continued with a diatribe against Jackson, saying, "I would sooner be honestly and politically damned, than hypocritically immortalized." He may have simply used the issue in his writing to bash Jackson once again. Noting that no remarks made by Crockett from the floor of the House either for or against Indian removal appear in the congressional record, Shackford concluded that Crockett did not actually oppose the removal of Indians to Oklahoma.

Other notables, however, did openly and publicly oppose the Indian Removal Bill. In June 1830, Sam Houston, a former congressman and governor of Tennessee, wrote in defense of the Indians. His article was published in the *Arkansas Gazette*. Houston had lived with the Cherokees for three years while an adolescent and later took refuge with them in Oklahoma after he resigned the governorship of Tennessee in April 1829 following an incident involving his 19-year-old bride of 11 weeks, who ran from their home screaming in the middle of the night.

It should be noted that, during the debate about Indian removal, some who supported the Indians also supported the federal intervention that led to their removal. It seems that the states—Georgia in particular—were treating the Indians so badly that placing them under the jurisdiction of the federal government was seen as more humane.

Witnessing Crockett's break with Jackson, powerful political factions decided to capitalize on his opposition. It seems that Jackson blamed the Second United States Bank for his defeat in 1824. After becoming president, he planned to curtail the power of that institution. The bank's president was Nicholas Biddle, who saw Crockett as a popular frontier figure who, if promoted properly, could defeat Jackson's supporters in Tennessee and undermine his political dominance. With that in mind, it appears that Biddle arranged for a friend, Matthew St. Clair Clarke, to befriend Crockett and to start molding the public's perception of the Tennessee congressman. To that end, biographer Shackford claimed that Clarke interviewed and traveled with Crockett so he could begin writing what was published in 1833 as *Life and Adventures of Colonel David Crockett of West Tennessee*. Crockett biographer Mark Derr contested this conclusion, declaring that James Strange French, not Clarke, was the author of the bogus biography. According to Derr, French used notes collected by Clarke, as well as other sources, including the contemporary play *The Lion of the West*.

Regardless of the authorship of the bogus biography, Clarke began to bring Crockett into the camp of the Eastern interests who opposed Jackson, according to Shackford. It should be noted that many, if not all, of Crockett's speeches and published materials were written by others on his behalf. Many of those pieces, more eloquently set down than he could have managed on his own, were written by Thomas Chilton, a fellow congressman who would help Crockett with his later autobiography, *A Narrative of the Life of David*

Crockett of the State of Tennessee. Many writers and biographers have suggested that Crockett was unaware of how he was being manipulated by these anti-Jackson factions.

There is ample evidence of such manipulation. Earlier in Crockett's career, when he was an outspoken Jackson man, the Whig newspapers had portrayed him as a bumbling backwoodsman who was too uncouth for polite society. He was considered a buffoon. Then, in November 1828, the *National Banner and Nashville Whig* printed a story about Crockett dining with President John Quincy Adams and being so ill-schooled in table manners that he drank from the finger bowl. When Crockett's reputation suffered and he asked for help in refuting the tale, the Whigs came to his rescue. Testimony from two prominent Whigs who were also at the dinner was published by the same paper in January 1829. When Whig papers defended Crockett against attacks and spoke of him in glowing terms, they helped mold the public's opinion of him, though their efforts were perhaps more strategic than truthful.

Crockett's constituents in West Tennessee were Jackson supporters. Crockett therefore had to tread very carefully around his loyalties. To the voters, he had to appear to be a Jackson man, while in Congress he had to appear in opposition. He apparently handled this dual role well. He was returned to Congress by a large margin in the 1829 election. This victory told Jackson supporters that they would have to work hard to remove Crockett from Congress.

In the campaign of 1831, the Whig papers played Crockett up to legendary stature. He did not object to the exaggerations. Meanwhile, the papers supporting Jackson focused on demeaning Crockett. They accused him of missing many votes in Congress, which was true. His accusers extended this fact into an accusation that Crockett had swindled the government by taking payment for attending Congress and then missing so many votes. They also criticized his break with Jackson and emphasized this to Crockett's pro-Jackson constituents in West Tennessee. To drive home their point, Jackson supporters would announce to the public that Crockett was to appear in a particular town on a particular day to explain his anti-Jackson position. They would then show up with circulars demeaning Crockett and pass them out to an audience that was already disappointed that Crockett was not there. By this under-handed technique, Jackson supporters undermined Crockett's base of support. Crockett also contributed to his own decline by losing some of his spirited campaign appeal. He no longer rolled with the punches his opponents dealt him but rather turned sour and vengeful in response. The people of West Tennessee could not respect a man who failed to weigh into a fight and hold his own.

During the 1831 campaign, Crockett's opponent, William Fitzgerald, made some outlandish and false charges. Crockett warned that if the falsehoods were repeated, he would personally thrash Fitzgerald. Fitzgerald was not discouraged. In Paris, Tennessee, Fitzgerald rose to speak and placed a handkerchief on the table before him. When he uttered the false charges, Crockett, against the advice of his handlers, rose from the audience and advanced. When Crockett was within a few feet, Fitzgerald pulled a pistol from beneath the handkerchief and stuck it in Crockett's face. Crockett stopped instantly in shock and surprise and, after a moment's thought, could only turn and retreat. His image among the citizenry was further diminished.

In the August 1831 election, Crockett was defeated. Though he carried a majority in 17 of his 18 counties, Madison County defeated him. He lost his seat in Congress by a margin variously reported as 586 votes or 807 votes. Crockett contested the count, to no avail. For the next two years, he remained as a private citizen on his homestead in West Tennessee, though he intended to run again and reclaim his seat.

Crockett was helped financially through his period out of office by loans from the Second United States Bank, of which Nicholas Biddle was president. Because Crockett could not repay the loans, they were forgiven. Biddle also forgave more extensive personal loans to other persons in powerful government positions, including many in Jackson's administration. One was Asbury Dickens, the chief clerk in the Treasury Department. Though historians have reached different conclusions about any criminal behavior implied by the writing off of such loans, questionable ethics and some degree of impropriety do seem to be suggested. In the minds of some, these arrangements cast aspersions on Crockett's character and reputation. Whether or not he understood the ramifications of his business dealings with Biddle is uncertain, but whatever alliances he made, he did so with the intention of getting legislation passed by Congress to help the poor frontier farmers of West Tennessee.

Crockett's stature on the national political scene was elevated by the writing and performing of the play *The Lion of the West*. This farce, based on an exaggerated Crockett-style character, took the stage in August 1831, just as Crockett lost his seat in Congress. Actor James Hackett played the lead role for two years in New York, then took the show to England. The play was written by James Kirke Paulding in pursuit of a prize offered by Hackett for an original American comedy. Paulding drew upon the image of Crockett that was already emerging in the public eye. Then, a year before performances began, the two creators went to great lengths to deny that the lead character, Colonel Nimrod Wildfire, was based on Crockett. As intended, this further strengthened the public's suspicions and reinforced what it thought it knew about David Crockett. According to biographer Mark Derr, James Strange

French borrowed material from the play to write *Life and Adventures of Colonel David Crockett of West Tennessee*. In December 1833, Crockett saw the play from a front-row seat and was applauded wildly by the audience, which recognized him and called out "Crockettisms" before the performance began. When Hackett took the stage, he bowed to the audience and then to Crockett. The audience again erupted in applause.

Crockett's prominence was also helped by the publication of *Life and Adventures of Colonel David Crockett of West Tennessee* in 1833. Of course, he was unable to publicly acknowledge its authorship or the part in the book's creation played by Eastern interests. In biographer Shackford's opinion, to have maximum impact on the citizens, the book had to appear as the writings of Crockett himself. However, as Crockett claimed not to have received any financial benefit from the book and to have immediately set out to write one of his own, it seems he may not have been a willing partner in the publication of *Life*. It was republished that same year under the title *Sketches and Eccentricities of Colonel David Crockett of West Tennessee*.

Perhaps this image-building worked in Crockett's favor. In the 1833 election, he won back his seat in Congress, narrowly beating the man who had defeated him two years earlier, William Fitzgerald (see the section on Trenton, Tennessee, pages 62-65). Crockett had regained the favor of his constituents despite his now-public break with Jackson.

Upon his return to Washington, Crockett found that much had transpired during his two-year absence and that new issues had arisen. Prominent among these was a battle over the rechartering of the Second United States Bank. President Jackson wanted to reduce that institution's influence because of its near-monopolistic power. In fact, since the bank had helped defeat him in the 1824 election, he would not have minded seeing it closed altogether. In an effort to defeat Jackson in the 1832 election, Nicholas Biddle had tightened credit and threatened economic ruin for the country. In retaliation, Jackson removed federal deposits from the bank. Because he did so by executive order while Congress was out of session in the fall of 1833, many returning congressmen were outraged at his presumptiveness and arrogance. Crockett was vocal among them, stating his intention to "return the deposits" should he be elected president. Crockett's alliance with the bank, which promised to help him enact his Tennessee Vacant Land Bill, may have helped motivate his anti-Jackson tirades. He spoke of Jackson as a despot and a usurper of powers rightly reserved for the people. At times, Crockett's opposition came across as emotional and unreasoned. He tried the patience of his fellow congressmen, wear-

The United States Capitol as it looks from Pennsylvania Avenue today.

ing thin their tolerance of his one-issue legislative focus.

Shortly after Congress convened in the late fall of 1833, Crockett submitted two motions regarding his land bill. He was perhaps naively optimistic about the bill's chance for passage. He had, he thought, many influential people working to promote his cause. In fact, his anti-Jackson associates were encouraging him to take a tour of the Eastern cities to help promote the sale of his forthcoming book, the autobiography *A Narrative of the Life of David Crockett of the State of Tennessee*. Though he hoped to do so during the congressional recess in 1834, the anti-Jackson faction arranged the tour while Congress was still in session. Some biographers believe that taking the tour while Congress was in session was Crockett's greatest political blunder. They claim it led directly to his downfall (see the section on Baltimore, Maryland, pages 170-79).

In the spring, after his tour of the East, Crockett sat for campaign portraits by John Gadsby Chapman. Each of the portraits represented a different aspect of the multifaceted Crockett. He liked the first painting enough to agree to do a full-length portrait, for which he posed as a frontier hunter complete with rifle and hunting dogs at his feet. Though Chapman had some pedigreed hounds he proposed to use, Crockett wanted three stray dogs brought in from the streets of Washington. They added authenticity, he said. Crockett posed almost daily from mid-May to the end of June, when he left for Philadelphia, where he planned to celebrate Independence Day (see the section on Philadelphia, Pennsylvania, pages 180-84). One of the Chapman paintings is displayed at the Alamo. The full-length portrait was the model for a statue of Crockett erected in Lawrenceburg, Tennessee, in 1922.

In the fall of 1834, Crockett returned to Washington after burying his father, John Crockett. In early December, he arranged for his Tennessee Vacant Land Bill to be first on the agenda, but that did not come to pass. He also introduced legislation for the clearing of the river channels in his district, but his congressional colleagues rejected his pleas even as he reduced the amount for which he was asking.

As Crockett's prowess at passing legislation declined, his personal finances reached a more urgent state. In December, he wrote to Nicholas Biddle asking for financial help regarding a previous debt. Eventually, Biddle wrote off the loan. Crockett also wrote his publisher to say that he was making good progress on the writing of a book about his tour of the Northeast the previous spring. He advised his publisher that he was delivering page after page to William Clark and boasted that he feared Clark would not be able to keep up with him. The urgency, of course, was that Crockett had a note due in a month and wanted an advance of $200 on the manuscript.

In the closing days of 1834, Crockett continued his attacks on Jackson. This time, he directed his venom at Jackson's apparent handpicked successor, Martin Van Buren, who was known as "The Little Magician" because he was short and politically shrewd. The presidential election was less than a year away. Crockett vowed that if Van Buren won, he, Crockett, would depart the country. Others had made the same declaration for political shock value, but Crockett was sincere. He said that if Van Buren were elected, "I will leave the united states for I never will live under this Kingdom before I will Submit to his government I will go to the wildes of Texas I will Consider that government a Paradice to what this will be."

During January and February 1835, Crockett tried again to bring his Tennessee Vacant Land Bill before the House of Representatives for a vote. He was unsuccessful. On his last attempt, as the congressional session was rapidly closing, his colleagues were unwilling to suspend the rules that would have allowed one last vote on the matter. As biographer Shackford concluded, "The House had apparently wearied of him, and his Eastern 'friends' had deserted."

On March 3, 1835, Crockett cast his last vote in Congress. It was on the losing side, in opposition to Jackson. The House adjourned that day, and Crockett returned to Tennessee for a summer of campaigning before the next election (see the section on Jackson, Tennessee, pages 56-62).

At age 13, Crockett visited Fells Point,
where he told a ship's captain he wanted to
work as a cabin boy for passage to London.

MARYLAND

Baltimore

Baltimore lies along Chesapeake Bay and the I-95 corridor
in Maryland northeast of Washington, D.C.

A few blocks east of the Inner Harbor is Fells Point, the
longtime center of shipbuilding and the shipping trade in the
Baltimore area dating back to 1726. A historic marker stands
in the market square at South Broadway and Thames Street.
An interpretive wayside exhibit is on the waterfront 100 feet
southwest of the marker. The Fells Point Maritime Museum at

1724 Thames Street interprets the history of the "world's fast-est ships"—the Baltimore clipper schooners—and the people who built and sailed them. Young David Crockett arrived at Fells Point in the spring of 1800.

Mount Vernon Place at Monument Square is the former site of Barnum's City Hotel, where Crockett stayed during his tour of the East in 1834. The hotel sat on the square surrounding the Washington Monument. It was razed in 1890.

The Baltimore & Ohio Railroad Museum displays locomo-tives and railroad cars from the earliest days of American railroading and gives visitors a good idea of the railroading experience Crockett had in 1834 as he left Baltimore. The museum is located at 901 West Pratt Street, not far from the Inner Harbor.

Ellicott City is about 10 miles west of the Inner Harbor along MD 144. It sits at the site of Ellicott Mills, established in 1772 along the historic National Road (MD 144) at the Patapsco River. A historic marker at Main Street (MD 144) and Oella Avenue on the east side of the Patapsco commemo-rates the mills and the considerable early economic activity along this section of the National Road.

David Crockett visited Baltimore twice, 34 years apart. In 1800, he was a young, uneducated boy running away from home, travel-ing by horse-drawn wagon on a dirt road and hoping to sail to Europe. In 1834, he was a United States congressman campaign-ing for national office, traveling by steamship and railroad to see the great cities of the Eastern seaboard. The contrast speaks to the dramatic changes that took place in Crockett's America dur-ing the first third of the 19th century.

In the spring of 1800, the 13-year-old Crockett was traveling from Gerrardstown to Baltimore with his wagoner companion, Adam Myers, who had promised Crockett a ride back to Tennessee (see the section on Gerrardstown, West Virginia, pages 155-56). As they neared Baltimore, they approached Ellicott Mills. Myers's horses were spooked by some workmen along the road who were pushing wheelbarrows. The horses bolted and "made a sudden wheel around," Crockett recalled. They "broke the wagon tongue slap, short off, as a pipe stem; and snap went both of the axletrees at the same time." Unfortunately, Crockett had chosen that time to be in the wagon, trying to change clothes among the barrels of flour they were hauling. He rattled around with the barrels but was not injured. He regarded his escape as fate, noting, "This proved to me, that if a fellow is born to be hung, he will never be drowned."

Myers used another wagon to haul the barrels and to tow their wreck for repair in Baltimore. Baltimore was the largest city Crockett had ever seen. While there, he roamed the waterfront at Fells Point, marveling at the tall ships and watching the hustle and bustle of the busy seaport. Fells Point was a community full of shipwrights, caulkers, laborers, stevedores, and draymen, all work-

Young David Crockett was changing clothes in the back of Adam Myers's wagon near the site of Ellicott Mills when the horses spooked and broke the wagon's axletrees.

ing at building ships and moving goods between warehouses and docks. It was a lively port with more than its share of temptations for a young man unfamiliar with such a place. Fells Point had at the time at least 47 taverns intended to slake the thirst and numb the monotony of those working on the waterfront.

During his visit, Crockett got up the nerve to board one of the ships, where he met the captain. The two talked for some time. The captain said he needed a cabin boy for his upcoming trip to London. He asked if Crockett would be interested and inquired as to what Crockett's parents would think. Crockett jumped at the opportunity, explaining that his parents were hundreds of miles away. He also thought that he had done well enough on his own that he was ready to make such a decision. He told the captain that he needed only to get his clothes and money and that he would return ready to depart on what he saw as a grand adventure.

When Crockett found Myers and explained his plan and why he needed his money, Myers flew into a rage and swore he would hold Crockett and return him to Tennessee. Crockett was surprised and disappointed. Myers kept a close watch on the boy for the next few days and threatened him with the wagon whip. Crockett could not get away. After the ship had sailed, however, Crockett decided he would make his escape whatever the consequences, with or without his money. Before dawn, he grabbed his clothing, stole away, and set out penniless.

Good fortune smiled upon the young man soon enough. Within two miles, he came upon a wagoner who was heading west. The man inquired of Crockett's situation. The kindness shown caused the lonely boy to burst into tears. After recovering his emotions, he explained about Adam Myers. The kindly wagoner, Henry Myers (no relation to Adam Myers), became quite angry about the injustice. He was, as Crockett described him, "a very large, stout-looking man, and as resolute as a tiger." Henry Myers told Crockett not to worry, that he would get the money or "whip it out of the wretch who had it," Crockett wrote.

Though Crockett was afraid to confront Adam Myers, Henry Myers took him along on the two-mile return trip. Henry Myers demanded the money from Adam Myers, who tried to blame Crockett at first but then confessed that he no longer had the money and had intended to repay it when they arrived back in Tennessee. Crockett was satisfied with the explanation and asked Henry Myers to drop the matter. They drove away, leaving Adam Myers alone.

Henry Myers and Crockett traveled together for several days before Crockett decided he wanted to head home at last. He planned to do so on foot. At an ordinary where several other wagoners were staying, Myers explained Crockett's plight and took up a collection to fund the young man's trip home. The group of kindhearted teamsters raised three dollars. Crockett set out the next morning determined to reach Tennessee and home (see the section on Radford, Virginia, pages 151-54).

Congressman David Crockett was a well-known figure by the time of his second visit to Baltimore. While Congress was still in session in April 1834—with important legislation still pending, including the appropriations bill—Crockett left Washington to make a three-week tour of Eastern and Northern cities for the supposed purpose of promoting his autobiography, *A Narrative of the Life of David Crockett of the State of Tennessee*, released by Carey & Hart of Philadelphia. With considerable help from his friend Thomas Chilton, a congressman from Kentucky, Crockett had during December 1833 and January 1834 written this account of his life to correct some of the exaggerations in the bogus biography published the year before under his name. With the release of Crockett's autobiography, however, biographer James Shackford claimed that Crockett's Whig associates were testing his appeal as a national political candidate. They planned a busy schedule for him through several Eastern cities so people might see for themselves the person they regarded as a "wild man from the West." This wild-man image had developed as a result of two literary efforts—one a book and the other a play. The book was *Life and Adventures of Colonel David Crockett of West Tennessee*, the bogus biography released in 1833, and the play was the comic farce *The Lion of the West*, which began playing in 1831 (see the section on Washington, District of Columbia, pages 157-69).

On April 25, Crockett set out from Washington by stagecoach for Baltimore. He took lodging there at Barnum's City Hotel on Mount Vernon Place (now Monument Square). In the ghost-written account of his tour, *An Account of Colonel Crockett's Tour of the North and Down East*, Crockett referred to the proprietor, David Barnum, as "Uncle Davie" and suggested a friendly relationship between the two. He took the opportunity to promote the establishment by saying, "No one need look for better quarters; if they do, it is

Monument Square in Baltimore was the site of Barnum's City Hotel, where Crockett stayed during his 1834 tour of the East.

because they don't know when they are satisfied."

After dinner and speeches that evening, Crockett left the next day by steamboat, crossing Chesapeake Bay. He then boarded a railroad car for the first time. "This was a clean new sight to me," he noted in the *Tour*. "About a dozen big stages hung on to one machine, and to start up hill. After a good deal of fuss, we all got seated and moved slowly off, the engine wheezing as if she had the *tizzick*. By-and-by she began to take short breaths, and away we went with a blue streak after us. The whole distance is seventeen miles, and it was run in fifty-five minutes."

Crockett took the railroad to Delaware City, then another steamboat up the Delaware River to Philadelphia, arriving on April 27. He stayed in the United States Hotel on Chestnut Street across from the Second United States Bank. Crockett was greeted in Philadelphia by a spirited group of young Whigs. After dinners, toasts, and speechmaking, they gave him a watch engraved with his "Go ahead" motto. Told that the young men also wished to make him a gift of a custom rifle, Crockett promised to return later to receive it. On April 28, he took a tour of the city including the waterworks, the mint, the navy hospital, the asylum, the exchange, the Girard School, and other places of note.

From Philadelphia on April 29, Crockett traveled to New York City by river and railroad through Perth Amboy. He was led about the city and asked to speak at every occasion. He attended the theater, visited the stock exchange, and toured the city's Sixth Ward, where he said unflattering things about the Irish residents there who supported Andrew Jackson. He attended banquets, met with newspaper editors, and agreed with Seba Smith, creator of the newspaper persona Major Jack Downing, that Crockett and Downing should exchange letters in a running column. On May 1, after much cajoling, Crockett attended an event in the Bowery for which his appearance had been advertised. Tired of giving speeches, he welcomed a trip to Jersey City on May 2, where he engaged in some target shooting.

From New York, Crockett traveled by water to Newport and then to Providence, Rhode Island, where he was cheered by a crowd. He then went by stage to Boston, where he stayed at the Tremont House on May 3. He subsequently received a tour of the textile-manufacturing plant of Amos Lawrence. Crockett was impressed by the cleanliness of the facility and the diligence of the several thousand women working there. Not understanding the labor issues involved, and contrasting what he saw to the conditions he knew in Tennessee and the South, Crockett surprised his guests at the evening's banquet in Lowell. He praised the women's opportunities and working conditions and declared that the protective tariff against which he had consistently voted would be welcomed by Southerners if they could see the economic opportunities it provided. This reversal of position befuddled many. But as some have pointed out, Crockett's practice was to say what was most appropriate for the audience he had at the moment.

An incident from *An Account of Colonel Crockett's Tour of the North and Down East* that took place in Boston illustrates the extent to which the author, William Clark, went to insert anti-Jackson propaganda. While in Boston, Crockett saw the USS *Constitution* in dry dock. According to the suspect account in the *Tour*, the workers had outfitted the bow with a new figurehead carved to look like Andrew Jackson. When asked if he thought it a good likeness, Crockett supposedly replied that he "had never seen him [Jackson] misrepresented; but, that they had fixed him just as he had fixed himself, that was, before the Constitution." Similarly contrived statements made the book unappealing to an audience wanting to read about the "wild man from the West."

After arriving in Providence on May 9, Crockett begged off a speaking engagement. From there, he returned to New York, then traveled to Camden, New Jersey, and Philadelphia. He returned to Baltimore on May 12 or 13 and arrived in Washington the day after.

During the remainder of May and most of June, while Crockett was involved with the business of the House of Representatives, he allowed the support he had received on his tour to embolden him to his own disadvantage. He became increasingly vocal in his opposition to Jackson and consequently less and less effective in Congress.

An Account of Colonel Crockett's Tour of the North and Down East was published in 1835 by Carey & Hart of Philadelphia. Though Crockett was credited as author, historians agree that the account was clearly not written by him. Just as the tour had a political agenda arranged by the Whigs, the book continued that ruse, filled as it was with pro-Whig and anti-Jackson propaganda using Crockett as the mouthpiece. Crockett contributed notes and gathered newspaper clippings about the itinerary, but the narrative was written by William Clark, a Whig congressman from Pennsylvania from 1833 to 1837. Biographer James Shackford declared that the book was "so inferior, so affectedly 'backwoodsie,' so full of sham vernacular and impossible harangue . . . that the *Tour* richly deserved the oblivion that it promptly received."

The third of Crockett's books, *The Life of Martin Van Buren, Hair-apparent to the "Government," and the Appointed Successor of General Jackson*, was also released in 1835. The spelling of *Heir* as *Hair* was perhaps a weak attempt to invoke the backwoods dialect readers expected of a book by Crockett, or it may have ridiculed Van Buren's baldness, which was accentuated by his bushy muttonchops. Though attributed to Crockett, the book was written by Judge Augustin Smith Clayton of Georgia as a political piece to support the candidacy of Judge Hugh Lawson White of Tennessee against Van Buren, the presumed presidential candidate for 1836. The book was too informed about national politics to have come from Crockett. Moreover, the author made no effort to imitate Crockett's unique phrasing or idioms. (For more information on Crockett's tenure as a congressman, see the section on Washington, District of Columbia, pages 157-69.)

Second United States Bank.
Photograph by Thomas L. Davies.
COURTESY OF INDEPENDENCE NATIONAL HISTORICAL PARK

PENNSYLVANIA

Philadelphia

Philadelphia sits along the I-95 corridor and the Delaware River in the southeast corner of Pennsylvania.

Independence National Historical Park, a unit of the National Park Service, interprets the history of the colonies' efforts to become free from British rule. The park includes several notable landmarks, including Independence Hall and the Liberty Bell. Near this historic section of Center City is the Second United States Bank on Chestnut Street, across from which stood the United States Hotel, where Crockett stayed in 1834.

The Hermitage Inn, site of a Fourth of July celebration attended by Crockett and 400 Whigs, was located 0.8 miles

> *south of Chestnut Street, following South Sixth Street and East Passyunk Avenue. "The Hermitage" was on the southwest corner of East Passyunk Avenue and Christian Street. Because the Whigs were gathering to lambaste Andrew Jackson, they may well have chosen the site simply to ridicule Jackson's Tennessee plantation home of the same name.*

On June 29, 1834, Congressman David Crockett departed Washington headed for home by way of Philadelphia. He planned to join Daniel Webster and a gathering of Whigs to spend Independence Day in Independence City bashing the reputation and the politics of President Andrew Jackson.

After spending the evening of June 29 in Baltimore, Crockett traveled by boat to Philadelphia on June 30. He stayed at the United States Hotel on Chestnut Street, across from the Second United States Bank. Before a crowd on July 1, the Whigs presented Crockett with a custom rifle, a tomahawk, and a butcher knife. According to Crockett, the presentation took place "in a room nearly fornent [opposite] the old statehouse." He spent the next day in Camden, New Jersey, shooting the new rifle. "I shot tolerable well, and was satisfied that when we became better acquainted, the fault would be mine if the varmints did not suffer," he wrote.

Crockett spent the next day fishing on the Schuylkill River. He joined a gathering at the well-known, historic Fish House, "where the fathers of our country, in ancient days, used to assemble and spend the day in taking their recreation and refreshments," Crockett wrote. "We amused ourselves shooting and catching perch. We had a nice refreshment, and abundance of the best to drink. Every gentleman took a hand in cooking; and the day was truly spent in harmony and peace."

On July 4, Crockett and several senators including Daniel Webster convened for festivities in Philadelphia. The citizens were greeted that day by "Remarks of Mr. Crockett of Tenn." printed in *The U.S. Gazette.* Knowing that the Whig rally was against "Executive usurpation" by President Jackson of Constitutional powers given others, Crockett railed against Jackson. He wrote passionately, and in part, "Sir it is useless to pass appropriation bills. A majority of this House has determined by their votes that Andrew Jackson shall be the Government. . . . We have seen him seize the Treasury of this country, and remove it from where the law had placed it. . . . I do not consider it good sense to be sitting here passing laws for Andrew Jackson to laugh at; it is not even good nonsense."

Crockett was among those who spoke at the Music Fund Hall early that day. "We were conducted up to the gallery in the first story of an immense building crowded below to overflowing with ladies and gentlemen," Crockett wrote. "After the address of the orator, the audience was also addressed by all the senators, and I was then called on. 'A speech from Colonel Crockett' was the cry all over the house. I was truly embarrassed to succeed so many great men, and where I saw so many ladies; but I found no excuse would do, and so spoke."

Later, the celebration continued at the Hermitage Inn, where Crockett arrived by carriage to loud cheers and cannon fire. He enjoyed the people and the "cool drinks of various kinds" until dinner was prepared. After toasts were made, the party was seated and served. Following dinner, Crockett asked the crowd to repair to the speaker's stand, where he addressed about 400 ladies and gentlemen. Webster and some of the other senators also spoke, and the audience enjoyed a reading of the Declaration of Independence. Upon the offering of more toasts at the tables, the evening concluded.

The Philadelphia Gazette reported on the occasion the following day. "First Congressional District. The Whigs of this district celebrated the anniversary of Independence by a public dinner at the Hermitage Inn. Before the company sat down, the Declaration of Independence was red [sic] by James Hanna, Esq. With much effect. . . .Col. Crocket[t] gave the citizens of the first district such a picture of the conduct and treatment abroad of their Representative, Joel B. Sutherland, as showed the latter in no very enviable light— –and one too that will be remembered by them in Oct. next."

Crockett then returned by carriage to Philadelphia and proceeded to the Chestnut Street Theater, where the second congressional district held its celebration. He was greeted by another enthusiastic crowd, which he entertained with a short address. According to biographer James Shackford, Crockett spoke about "tyranny, sword, purse, despotism, and independence." At the conclusion of the address, he retreated to the United States Hotel. Crockett wrote that he could not have given three speeches in such a short span except for the setting and the occasion: "I was stimulated by being in sight of the old State-house, and Independence square, where the fathers of our county met, as it were, with halters on their necks, and subscribed their names to that glorious Declaration of Independence."

After resting on July 5, Crockett received on July 6 a gift of several canisters of gunpowder from the noted chemist and powder maker E.I. du Pont de Nemours, whom Crockett referred to as "Mr. Dupont." E. I. du Pont was a director on the board of the Second Bank of the United States.

The next day, Crockett began his journey home to Tennessee with a train ride west from Philadelphia toward Pittsburgh. He passed through Columbia in Lancaster County, where he stopped for a few minutes. The archives of Lancaster County hold this account of Crockett's appearance: "He went 'ahead,' after a delay of fifteen minutes, and leaving persons who expected to see a wild man of the woods clothed in a hunting shirt and covered with hair, a good deal surprised at having viewed a respectable looking personage, dressed decently and wearing his locks much after the fashion of our plain German farmers."

At Pittsburgh, he boarded the *Hunter* and steamed down the Ohio River to Wheeling, Virginia (now West Virginia), where he refused the opportunity to speak but endured the captain's taking the boat back upriver so he could come around again and enable the crowd to send Crockett off with a rousing cheer.

He arrived in Cincinnati on July 12, a Saturday. He gave a speech and then continued to Louisville on July 13, where he spoke to crowds several times. He also spoke in Jeffersonville Springs, Indiana.

In a few days, he caught the steamboat *Scotland* and proceeded downriver to Mills Point, Tennessee. There, his second son, William, met him for the 35-mile ride home to the Obion River country (see the section on Rutherford, Tennessee, pages 65-82).

The Hinderliter Grog Shop, the oldest building in Little Rock, interprets tavern life on the Arkansas frontier of the 1830s.

ARKANSAS

Little Rock

Little Rock, the capital of Arkansas, is in the center of the state along the Arkansas River where I-40 intersects I-30.

The Historic Arkansas Museum is located at 200 East Third Street. On the museum's one city block are houses built before 1836, the days of the Arkansas Territory. The Hinderliter Grog Shop is the oldest structure in Little Rock. Tradition and a marker erected in 1936 by the Daughters of the American Revolution at the northwest corner of Third and Cumberland streets say that this building was the site of the last meeting of the Arkansas Territorial Legislature, from October 5 through November 19, 1835. Lacking historic documentation, the museum does not make this claim. David Crockett arrived in Little

Rock on Thursday, November 12, of that year. The museum is also home to the 1821 print shop of William Woodruff, owner of the Arkansas Gazette, the oldest newspaper in continuous operation west of the Mississippi River. A replica of his wooden Ramage press and other artifacts, including his desk and chair, are on the premises. Woodruff wrote and published accounts of Crockett's visit to Little Rock and later of his death at the Alamo. The museum's galleries include the American Bladesmith Society Hall of Fame and an extensive exhibit of Bowie knives. The Bowie knife was created by James Black in Washington, Arkansas.

The Old State House Museum is located at 300 West Markham Street. Under construction at the time Crockett passed through Little Rock, the statehouse opened in 1836 for the first session of the Arkansas State Legislature.

The Jeffries Hotel, sometimes called the City Hotel, was located near the Old State House. This was the site where Crockett entertained local notables who gathered to host a dinner in his honor. Some territorial legislators were probably among them.

In November 1835, David Crockett and his three companions left his home in West Tennessee bound for Texas. Along their way through Jackson, Tennessee, they learned of the conflict in Texas and picked up a number of volunteers wanting to join in their ride west. After a night of drinking in Memphis, the party of travelers, perhaps then numbering several more than when Crockett left home, crossed the Mississippi River and headed west toward Texas. The men most likely followed a military road built in the late 1820s. A map from 1836 shows this road passing through Marion and St. Francis, then continuing to Little Rock.

In the early 1830s, Arkansas was a rough frontier, and Little Rock was a hamlet of only a few hundred people. The rude cabins were shuttered affairs with no glass in the windows. Many of the people in the territory came to hunt bears, which were plentiful in the early 1800s. Others were escaping the law in other states. Regardless of their motives, they arrived in Little Rock and took lodging at establishments such as the Hinderliter Grog Shop, where they ate, drank, and gambled. Indicative of the character of the country was the common name for a deck of playing cards—"an Arkansas Bible." Crockett was no stranger to such harshness, having experienced life as a young drover on the roads of Tennessee and Virginia some 35 years earlier.

As the riders approached the small frontier town that would become the new state's capital the following year, Crockett shot a deer at a good distance, using Old Betsy, his trusted firearm. (Pretty Betsy, a rifle given him by the Whigs in Philadelphia in 1834, remained at home in Tennessee.) Crockett brought the kill with him into town, then set about butchering it behind the Jeffries Hotel, where he was staying. Soon recognized by members of the community, he was invited that evening to a dinner in his honor at the hotel.

Crockett's presence in Little Rock was newsworthy. The dinner was attended by community notables, who came to see the famous frontiersman and to have Crockett entertain them. He spoke against Jackson, knowing that some members of his audience were anti-Jackson. He talked about political conflicts in Washington and about Texas independence, among other subjects. The newspapers noted that in the week after he spoke, four local men set off for Texas, apparently inspired by Crockett's patriotic fervor.

William Woodruff reported on the dinner in the next issue of the *Arkansas Gazette*, noting that "Col. David Crockett—better known as Davy Crockett—the raal [real] critter himself," had arrived in town with six or eight followers. He said that Crockett's men were "on their way to Texas, to join the patriots of that country in freeing it from the shackles of the Mexican government." Such a contemporary report supports author Manley Cobia's deduction that Crockett added to his objectives for going to Texas after he left his Tennessee home. Confirming Crockett's celebrity, Woodruff's report added that "hundreds flocked to see the wonderful man, who, it is said, can whip his weight in wild-cats, or grin the largest panther out of the highest tree."

Crockett was not in Little Rock very long. Having arrived on Thursday, the day of the dinner, he left on Friday morning. Despite the brevity of his stay, legends of Crockett's exploits in Arkansas abounded, including tales about his marksmanship and bear hunting. He was a national figure, and his name was used to gain the ear of an audience for one story and another. Moreover, the *Crockett Almanacs*, which exploited his personage most egregiously after he died, had already begun. Charles Ellms, a Boston illustrator, issued the first in 1835 through publisher Snag and Sawyer of Nashville. It was called *Davy Crockett's Almanack of Wild Sports of the West, and Life in the Backwoods*. Various publishers issued others in the following years. These comic works of fantasy reinforced the mythical Crockett as a rip-roarin' backwoodsman—the image he had written his autobiography to help dispel. Nevertheless, these annual collections, printed from 1835 to 1856, more effectively than any other effort formed the public's image of the man. In the early issues, he was portrayed as a comic superhuman frontiersman with fantastical abilities. In the later issues, his character was usurped to promote territorial expansionism; he was portrayed as a racist and as crude, harsh, and sexual.

During his brief visit to Little Rock, Crockett was exposed to news coming from Texas. Letters from Sam Houston and Stephen Austin had been printed in recent issues of local papers. Houston wrote, "Let each man come with a good rifle, and one hundred rounds of ammunition, and to come soon." Austin wrote of a gathering of several hundred volunteers intending to capture San Antonio (known as Béxar in Crockett's day), the site of the Alamo. Manley Cobia concluded that when Crockett left Little Rock, he had a specific destination in mind and was eager to get there. The *Arkansas Advocate*, a rival paper of the *Gazette*, said Crockett departed Little Rock "armed from head to foot" and "amid the huzzas of men, women, girls, and boys." Having left Tennessee in search of new land for his family, Crockett was now riding off to war (see the next section on Washington, Arkansas).

The statehouse was under construction and near the Jeffries Hotel in 1835.

Old Washington Historic State Park straddles the Old Southwest Trail, which Crockett took to Texas.

Washington

Washington is on US 278 about nine miles northwest of Hope, which is located at Exit 30 off I-30 in southwest Arkansas. Old Washington Historic State Park is on US 278 (Columbus Street) in Washington. The park interprets the history of this major community on the early Arkansas frontier. The tavern where David Crockett stayed no longer exists. However, the oldest building in town dates to 1836, the year after he passed through on his way to Texas. Franklin Street (AR 195) is believed to follow the route of the Old Southwest Trail. It leads 14 miles southwest to Fulton.

Blacksmith James Black created the Bowie knife in Washington when Jim Bowie lived here around 1830.

In mid-November 1835, David Crockett and his party of Texas-bound adventurers rode out of Little Rock along the Old Southwest Trail. This military road, used to move the Choctaws to Western lands, was built on an old buffalo trace. An 1836 map shows the road connecting Little Rock, Benton, Rockport (Malveun), Blakely Town, Greenville, Washington, and Fulton.

After about 125 miles, the riders arrived in Washington. Author Manley Cobia suggested that, there and along the way, Crockett stopped to visit old friends. James Nichols was a boy when his father knew Crockett in East Tennessee. Armstead Blevins, whose family claimed in later years that Crockett spent a week hunting deer with him, also lived nearby. Cobia was suspicious of this family tradition about a week-long hunt, as he felt Crockett was eager to get to Texas. Once in Washington, Crockett probably rested at the Washington Tavern on the Old Southwest Trail (now Franklin Street).

From Washington, Crockett's party continued southwest toward Texas. The exact route is unknown. Cobia identified a couple of possible routes, including one suggesting a leisurely steamboat ride to Natchitoches, probably from Fulton, which was a steamboat stop on the Red River. The route favored by many historians, including biographer James Shackford and Cobia, would have taken Crockett from Washington to Fulton, where the party would have ridden by horseback along the north side of the Red River into what is now Oklahoma. There, the men crossed the Red River at Jonesboro, north of Clarksville (see the section on Clarksville, Texas, pages 195-200).

David Crockett is credited with naming De Kalb for a hero of the American Revolution.

De Kalb

De Kalb sits on US 82 in Bowie County in the northeast corner of Texas. The intersection of US 82 and Runnels Street marks the center of town. A commemorative plaque is on the west side of town on Northwest Fulton Street 0.3 mile along US 82 from Runnels Street. It declares that the town was named for Major General Johann De Kalb, a hero of the American Revolution, at the suggestion of David Crockett, who was passing through the area.

De Kalb sits along the route David Crockett most likely took as he returned in early 1836 from an impromptu hunting expedition while en route to San Antonio, then called Béxar (see the section on Clarksville, pages 195-200). Having found the western route as intimidating as he had been warned it would be, Crockett led his party of riders east to find Trammel's Trace, which would take them south to Nacogdoches.

Several historic markers in Texas commemorate Trammel's Trace. One sits on US 71 some 1.5 miles north of I-30 in Texarkana. Another, missing at the time of this writing, was along US 59 in Jefferson in Marion County. A third was erected in Tatum near the Rusk County-Panola County line on TX 149 a quarter-mile south of TX 43.

Trammel's Trace was established in 1813. It connected the Old Southwest Trail from St. Louis with El Camino Real (the King's Highway) into Mexico (see the section on Nacogdoches, Texas, pages 202-8).

The Trammel's Trace marker in Tatum is one of several in East Texas marking the historic route from Texarkana to Nacogdoches.

David Crockett crossed the Red River into Texas at Jonesboro, commemorated today along FM 410.

Jonesboro Crossing

Twenty-seven driving miles north-northwest of Clarksville in far northeast Texas, a well-maintained display of markers and a historic grave commemorate the history of Jonesboro, where many early settlers and historic figures entered Texas by crossing the Red River. From US 82 in Clarksville, proceed north on TX 37 for 18 miles. Just south of the Red River bridge, go west on FM (farm road) 195 for 2.5 miles to FM 410. Follow FM 410 north for 6.6 miles to the roadside park and commemorative display, on the right.

Established by ferryman Henry Jones in 1815, Jonesboro was a major hub of activity in the early 19th century. The farthest navigable point upstream on the Red River, it was also a terminus of Trammel's Trace, or at least a feeder trail to the trace. Trammel's Trace ran south to Nacogdoches. A steamship port, a hotel, and a blacksmith shop served the people coming into Texas at Jonesboro. At one time, the community was home to about 2,300 souls.

Jonesboro also served as the county seat of Miller County, which at the time included parts of what are now northeast Texas, southwest Arkansas, and Oklahoma. It was likely at this crossing that David Crockett and Texas legends Sam Houston and Stephen Austin entered Texas. In 1843, a flood wiped out the town and moved the Red River channel a mile away. Jonesboro, which had already been losing trade to other towns, soon disappeared.

According to author Manley Cobia, Jr., Crockett may have crossed into Texas in 1835 at one of four different places. All have been credibly suggested by historians. The crossing at Jonesboro seems most probable and is commemorated as such by a marker. From here, Crockett and his party rode south in search of the home of William Becknell (see the next section on Clarksville).

Clarksville

Clarksville is the county seat of Red River County in extreme northeast Texas, bordering Oklahoma. It sits at the intersection of US 82 and TX 37. A marker for the site of the William Becknell home is along US 82 some 3.9 miles west of the town square.

In 1835, Red River County was formed from Miller County. The new county seat was established at Clarksville (also known as Fort Clark), a town built in 1833 by James Clark and his wife, Isabella, who moved here from Jonesboro, about 22 miles north. Clark provided the land for the first courthouse, which sat on what is now the town square.

David Crockett and his party crossed the Red River at Jonesboro in 1835. At that point, they may or may not have still been in the

United States. The Red River Valley was disputed territory, both the United States and Mexico claiming jurisdiction. The Sabine River, to the south, was the border accepted by most Americans.

Crockett and his party rode southeast from Jonesboro and reportedly spent their first night in Texas at the home of John Stiles in White Rock, about eight miles east-northeast of Clarksville. They soon passed near, if not directly through, Clarksville. Crockett was searching for the home of William Becknell, a man he either already knew or wanted to meet because of his reputation on the frontier. Becknell, who had moved to the area from Missouri, was the man who had established the Santa Fe Trail, which allowed trade between the United States and New Spain in the West. During the War of 1812, while Crockett was riding with General Andrew Jackson in the Mississippi Territory (what is now Alabama), Becknell served as a United States mounted ranger under Captain Daniel Morgan Boone in Missouri. Boone was the son of famous pioneer Daniel Boone, in whose honor Crockett had named his Bean's Creek home "Kentuck" (see the section on Maxwell, Tennessee, pages 41-46).

The party received directions to Becknell's home from a man who later that day told Isabella Clark about his chance meeting with the famous David Crockett. Mrs. Clark, then 31, knew that the party was riding into danger, as Comanches were raiding in the area toward which Crockett was traveling. Wasting no time, she jumped on her horse and rode to the spot where her informer said he had met Crockett's party. From there, she could easily follow the trodden grass left by their passing. Upon arriving at the Latimer home, she was joined by Jane and Betty Latimer in her search for Crockett.

Accounts differ on exactly where the women overtook the Crockett party. Perhaps it was at the Becknell home, though that would not have been very far away. They advised the men of the danger ahead. Though not ungrateful for the effort made on their behalf, Crockett and his party continued riding west the next morning for about 20 miles as the women turned back toward Clarksville.

At the end of that day's ride, Crockett's party made camp in what is now downtown Paris in Lamar County. A Paris street is named Crockett Circle to honor the approximate location of the camp. Crockett Circle intersects Clarksville Street between 19th and 20th streets in the southeast quarter of town. No historic marker is on the site.

In the morning, the men rode through what would become the heart of Paris, where they met a family who advised them against continuing south or west. The man of the family told the riders that little game was available to the west to sustain them. He recommended they turn around and ride east along the more well-traveled route to Nacogdoches and then to San Antonio (known at that time as Béxar). Again, Crockett and his fellow travelers continued west and south on what they believed was a faster route to reach William Travis and the volunteers assembling for a fight.

William Becknell was living on the edge of the prairie when Crockett stopped to visit soon after entering Texas.

Continuing south to the headwaters of the Trinity River near what is now Dallas, Crockett's party came upon a group of riders heading north. Some accounts suggest it was a party sent from Clarksville to drive the Comanches away. When told of the brave women who had come to warn Crockett's party, the men returning from the plains readily declared that they could have been led only by Isabella Clark. Crockett was again warned of the difficulty of proceeding south and west through the open, spare wilderness.

The exact details of the next part of the odyssey are not recorded. Historian Manley Cobia suggested that the party split about that time. Some of the men, near starvation, returned east ahead of the others. Eventually, Crockett also turned back east. At that point, he was probably traveling with only three men.

Crockett and his party turned northeast and headed for Clarksville, rather than retracing their previous steps. Along this return trip, Crockett came upon a grove of trees surrounded by prairie grass. His party found some hollow trees filled with wild bees and honey. Later, Crockett wrote a letter home praising the area and declaring that he planned to move there. He called it Honey Grove (see the next section on Honey Grove).

Crockett and his men continued east toward the Becknell home, where they met Henry Stout, a legendary hunter and guide. Stout took the party on an expedition west to an area referred to as Choctaw Bayou, where the hunting was superb. Some historians have suggested that Crockett's reference to "the Border" area in a letter he wrote shortly afterward may have been to Bois d'Arc Creek. Both Choctaw Bayou and Bois d'Arc Creek are along the Red River downstream of what are now Lake Texoma and the Denison Dam, over which runs US 75. These areas are 90 to 100 miles west of the Becknell home near Clarksville.

Rumors about Crockett spread throughout Texas. Some said he

had been killed by the Comanches. Later found to be hunting, Crockett was criticized by some for forgetting his declared intention of coming to Texas to fight for its freedom. Edward Warren, visiting Texas from Bangor, Maine, wrote home, "You may have heard that David Crockett set out for this country with a company of men to join the army. He has forgotten or waved his original intention & stopped some 80 or 100 miles to the north of this place to hunt Buffalo for the winter! For a long time, it was feared that he & his party had been destroyed by the tribes of wild Indians through which he intended to pass. But, at last, it is ascertained that he is at his favorite amusement."

Arriving in Clarksville a few weeks after Crockett was Mansil W. Matthews, a teacher, physician, and preacher. Matthews had led a group of settlers from Alabama to Texas. On his recent journey from Jackson, Tennessee, Crockett had ridden with Matthews as far as Memphis. Perhaps because the preacher stopped every Sunday during his trip, Crockett had left the slow-moving group, crossing the Mississippi and riding ahead into Arkansas. In Clarksville, Matthews held the first Church of Christ service in Texas on January 17, 1836. By that date, Crockett had already made his way south to Nacogdoches.

Crockett's route from Clarksville to Nacogdoches after his return from hunting with Stout has been explored by several historians. He probably rode east to Trammel's Trace. Some accounts say that, along the way, he stopped at the home of Colin McKinney in what is now Bowie County, where he suggested the name for the community of De Kalb. He later stopped at Lost Prairie, Arkansas, on the west side of the Red River, where he traded his watch for that of Dr. Isaac Newton Jones plus $30. Crockett needed the money. Dr. Jones would later return the watch with a letter to Elizabeth Crockett in what may have been her first news of her husband's plight at the Alamo.

From Lost Prairie, Crockett rode south and probably crossed the Sabine River at Logansport, where the river enters Louisiana. During the first week of January 1836, he followed the Spanish Trail southwest to Nacogdoches, where he caught up on news of the rapidly changing political events in Texas (see the section on Nacogdoches, pages 202-8).

Honey Grove

The community of Honey Grove sits at the intersection of US 82 and TX 34/TX 50 in Fannin County some 22 miles west-southwest of Paris. Crockett Park is between Main and Market streets one block west of TX 34/TX 50. A historical marker is on West Market Street.

This is the site named by David Crockett in a letter to family and friends near the end of his life (see the section on Clarksville, pages 195-200). One legend says that Crockett carved his name into a tree in the grove. Another says he carved the words *Honey Grove*. In either case, he found the site delightful. In fact, he said he planned to return to the area to settle.

The grove is thought to have been just north of what is now the town square about a half-mile northeast of Crockett Park.

The smallest state park in Texas at ¹/₁₀₀ acre,
Elizabeth Patton Crockett Acton State Historic
Site marks the grave of Crockett's second wife.
COURTESY TEXAS PARKS AND WILDLIFE DEPARTMENT

Acton

Acton is southwest of Dallas-Fort Worth in Hood County. It
is about nine miles east of Granbury off US 377 at the inter-
section of FM (farm road) 167 and FM 4. Elizabeth Patton
Crockett Acton State Historic Site is located in the town's
cemetery.

In 1853, the state of Texas issued a land warrant to Elizabeth Patton Crockett for her martyred husband's service in the war for Texas independence. She was awarded 1,280 acres in north Texas, where Indian attacks were still common. She arranged for a surveyor, who bargained for half the land, given the risk involved. That left her with 640 acres on Rucker's Creek. Some accounts say she received a parcel of 640 acres, which was cut in half in the bargain. However, the enticement to freedom fighters in the Texas

Revolution was "a league and a labor" of land. A league was two square miles—that is, 1,280 acres. A labor, or *labrado*, was a small garden plot.

Elizabeth Crockett moved to Texas with her son Robert and daughter Matilda. She lived there for seven years in a log cabin, always wearing black, as she had since learning of Crockett's death in 1836. On January 31, 1860, at the age of 72, she left the cabin for a walk and collapsed dead. She was buried in the Acton Cemetery.

Elizabeth Patton Crockett Acton State Historic Site is the smallest state park in Texas, at 12 feet by 21 feet. The 28-foot marble monument of a bonneted pioneer woman shading her eyes to scan the horizon, looking for her husband's return, was unveiled in 1913.

Nacogdoches

Nacogdoches is in Nacogdoches County in East Texas at the intersection of US 59 Business and TX 21. It bills itself as the "Oldest Town in Texas." Main Street (TX 21) follows the route of the Old San Antonio Road and El Camino Real (the King's Highway).

The Old Stone Fort, where David Crockett took the Oath of Allegiance, sat at Main and Fredonia streets where the Commercial Bank of Texas is today. A plaque on the bank building commemorates the fort. An adjacent DAR marker honors the King's Highway. Across Main Street is the Historic Town Center, which offers exhibits and displays about Nacogdoches history. A statue of Antonio Gil Ybarbo, builder of the Old Stone Fort in 1779, stands next to the center. A statue of Thomas J. Rusk, the first secretary of war for the new Republic of Texas, is at North Street across Main Street from the center. When Crockett passed through town, Rusk bought two of his rifles.

North of downtown along US 59 Business is the campus of Stephen F. Austin State University, which is home to a 1936 replica of the Old Stone Fort that serves as a museum. It is located on Griffith Boulevard at Clark Boulevard (Alumni Drive).

Farther north just off US 59 Business is Millard's Crossing Historic Village on Old Post Oak Road. The village displays relocated historic buildings, including some from the time when Crockett rode through Nacogdoches.

Two blocks east of the Historic Town Center is the Sterne-Hoya House at East Pilar Street and Lanana Street. Crockett stayed in the home of Nicholas Adolphus Sterne during his visit. Sterne outfitted the New Orleans Greys, who fought in the Texas Revolution. One company camped in the peach orchard in front of his home.

One block north of the Sterne-Hoya House is Eugenia Sterne Park, which is home to a statue called The Treaty. It commemorates the negotiation of a temporary peace with Indian tribes who otherwise could have complicated the Texans' fight against the Mexicans. Sam Houston and Chief Bowles are portrayed.

One block east of Eugenia Sterne Park on TX 21 at Lanana Creek is a marker commemorating the Old San Antonio Road. The historic route ran east for 30 miles to San Augustine, where Crockett was greeted warmly by the settlers.

In the fall of 1835, David Crockett and his party of travelers attempted to make their way to San Antonio to join in the fight for Texas independence as they understood it. Political circumstances changed rapidly after Crockett left Tennessee. By January 1836, when he arrived in Nacogdoches, he learned of the new situation. The leaders of Texas were meeting and corresponding in a rather confusing effort to establish some sense of order to their revolutionary effort and to amass an army of either regulars or volunteers. The councilmen were pledging money the revolutionary government did not have and declaring broad and often contradictory positions, which were then ignored or countered by others. It was a desperate time.

Despite the muddled plans of the leaders, the call for volunteers to come to Texas, as Crockett was doing, was bringing others as well. Many were convening in Nacogdoches. There, they heard news of events elsewhere. Often, that news was weeks old.

When Crockett arrived in Nacogdoches, very likely on January 5, 1836, a banquet given by the women of the town was under way to honor a champion of the revolution, Don Agustin Viesca. Recognized when he entered town, Crockett was brought to the banquet hall, where he was cheered vigorously. He spoke to the gathering as an enthusiastic patriot and backwoods hunter, saying, according to one eyewitness account, "We'll go to the city of Mexico and shake Santa Anna as a coon dog would a possum." A report in the *Nile's Weekly Register* of April 9 offered another account: "The old bear-hunter . . . began nearly in this style, 'I am told, gentlemen, that, when a stranger, like myself, arrives among you, the first inquiry is—what brought you here? To satisfy your curiosity at once as to myself, I will tell you all about it. I was, for some years, a member of Congress. In my last canvass, I told the people of my district, that, if they saw fit to reelect me, I would serve them faithfully as I had done; but, if not, they might go to h___, and I would go to Texas. I was beaten, gentlemen, and here I am.' The roar of applause was like a thunder-burst."

Like many other volunteers arriving in Nacogdoches, Crockett took the Oath of Allegiance. It is uncertain whether he did so upon his arrival at Nacogdoches during the first week of January or perhaps as much as nine days later, after returning from a visit to the nearby community of San Augustine. In any event, when asked to take the oath at the Old Stone Fort in the presence of its author, Judge John J. Forbes, Crockett altered it slightly, declaring that he would support only a "republican" government. Some historians have written that Crockett still believed that President Andrew Jackson was usurping powers not given him by the Constitution. With that in mind, and knowing that Santa Anna had disregarded the Mexican Constitution of 1824 and become a dictator, Crockett may have wanted to declare his unwillingness to fight for a despotic leader. Author Manley Cobia, Jr., suggested that Crockett, in the midst of being celebrated, demanded the alteration simply to be different and to make himself the center of attention. According to Cobia, all the other volunteers signing the oath appeared to

Crockett signed the Oath of Allegiance at the Old Stone Fort, a replica of which is nearby today.

understand that it supported the type of government in force in the United States.

Crockett had left his Tennessee home in the company of two family members and a neighbor. Somewhere along the way, Abner Burgin and Lindsey Tinkle separated from Crockett and returned home. They may have ridden into Nacogdoches with Crockett. The only certainty is that they did not sign the Oath of Allegiance. William Patton, accepted by many historians as Crockett's nephew, did sign the oath. Others also signed it and joined Colonel Crockett's company. Historians generally accept a list of 16 men who rode with Crockett as volunteers. Adding to his letter begun in San Augustine on January 9, Crockett informed his family that he had joined the army, taken an "oath of government," as he called it, and was heading for the Rio Grande in a few days.

On January 15, his horse, rifle, and equipment were placed into the service of Texas at a value of $240. Though Crockett may have left Little Rock "heavily armed," as was reported in the newspaper, he apparently ran short of cash along the way. He sold two rifles to Thomas Jefferson Rusk in Nacogdoches for $60. From the accounts of others in the party, Crockett and his men were awaiting a band of volunteers from Columbia, Tennessee. After that band arrived, the men planned to ride 125 miles to Washington to await General Sam Houston and to serve as auxiliary volunteers in the capacity he directed.

Many writers have speculated on Crockett's motivation for joining the volunteers. He had declared in a letter before leaving Tennessee that he wanted to explore Texas. He was clearly looking to build the personal wealth that had eluded him into his 50th year. Along the way, he became enamored with the notion of fighting for freedom in another revolution. Upon his arrival, Crockett was greeted by crowds that had read newspaper accounts of his intent to fight in Texas. It may also be that, after hearing some Texans invite him to represent them at their Constitutional Convention, Crockett experienced a rebirth of his desire to be part of a new government (see the next section on San Augustine). As Cobia pointed out, for a man who had only recently considered himself a viable candidate for president of the United States, Crockett may have envisioned himself as a major leader—perhaps president—of a future Republic of Texas. He needed to attend the Constitutional Convention to put himself in that position. To do so, he needed a community of support. According to Cobia, Crockett joined the army in part to win the support of the other volunteers, who might then champion his participation in the convention. Cobia's image of Crockett suggests an opportunist not so much interested in fighting for independence as in earning the support of a constituency for the new republic that would follow the revolution.

Winning a seat at the Constitutional Convention would depend on elections to be held February 1. It was unclear, however, who

Crockett stayed with Nicholas Adolphus Sterne while in Nacogdoches.

Sam Houston and Chief Bowles are portrayed in The Treaty *at Eugenia Sterne Park.*

was eligible to vote. One ordinance said that "all free white males and Mexicans" could vote, but local residency was a requirement, too. In spite of this, the volunteers coming to fight wanted to vote. When they were told they could not, one group of Kentucky volunteers took positions outside the Old Stone Fort and threatened to open fire. The judge, presumed to be Forbes, asked for a show of hands among the local citizenry regarding the Kentuckians' right to vote. When the citizens said no, the judge had to intervene to calm the volunteers thus rebuffed. Then, to everyone's surprise, Forbes allowed them to vote. In celebration, the soldiers paraded about town in a raucous manner, making the citizens fearful (see the section on Crockett, pages 211-12).

Some citizens of San Augustine, located along the Old San Antonio Road, asked Crockett to be their delegate to the Constitutional Convention.

San Augustine

San Augustine is located 30 miles east of Nacogdoches along TX 21, the Old San Antonio Road. A marker in the parking lot of the chamber of commerce, a half-mile east on TX 21 from US 96, commemorates the Old San Antonio Road. An identical marker is in Nacogdoches on TX 21 at Lanana Creek. Today, TX 21 from Nacogdoches to San Augustine is part of the Texas Forest Trail.

A marker four miles east of San Augustine on TX 21 commemorates the homesite of Elijah Roberts, where David Crockett stayed for a few days.

After a day or two in Nacogdoches in early January 1836, David Crockett rode east along the Old San Antonio Road some 30 miles to a new town named San Augustine. It had been established three years earlier in defiance of the Spanish Royal Ordinance of 1563, which stipulated how towns were to be laid out. Because it recognized English as its primary language and developed a business district along Main Street, rather than on a square, this town was unique among Texas settlements. It was also unique in its welcome of Crockett, who was greeted by an official firing of the town's cannon. A banquet was held in his honor as well. Many believe that his reception at this decidedly Anglo community was the grandest Crockett received in Texas.

Crockett remained a few days at the home of Elijah Roberts, formerly of East Tennessee. Part of a community called the Tennessee Colony, Roberts lived a few miles east of San Augustine at Old Brick Springs. Roberts had also hosted notables Sam Houston, William Travis, and Jim Bowie at his home. On January 9 at San Augustine, Crockett began writing to his daughter the only letter that survives from his Texas expedition.

Crockett was encouraged by the citizens of San Augustine to serve as a candidate for the Constitutional Convention, to be held in the town of Washington in March. He declined to run but expected to be elected anyway. He wrote home to Margaret with enthusiasm, "I have but little doubt of being elected a member to form a Constitution for this province. I am rejoiced at my fate. I had rather be in my present situation than to be elected to a seat in Congress for life. I am in hopes of making a fortune yet for myself and family bad as my prospect has been."

Crockett returned to Nacogdoches by January 15 (see the section on Nacogdoches, pages 202-8).

Mistaken for a horse thief, Crockett was saved from hanging by his old Tennessee friend Elijah Gossett, who lived here.

Crockett

Crockett, the county seat of Houston County, is located southwest of Nacogdoches at the intersection of US 287 and TX 21. A historic marker on the town square mentions the naming of the town to honor David Crockett. A marker commemorating the home of Elijah Gossett is two miles east of the town square on TX 21.

Following the Old San Antonio Road southwest toward Washington, David Crockett and his party of 16 men left Nacogdoches on or after January 15, 1836, to join the fight for Texas independence. They departed before an expected group of volunteers arrived from Columbia, Tennessee (see the section on Nacogdoches, pages 202-8). The Old San Antonio Road and El Camino Real, also known as the King's Road (TX 21), share the same route in places and take different routes in others.

Some 80 miles west of Nacogdoches, Crockett and a couple of his riders must have separated from the group and made their own camp. While there, they were mistaken for local horse thieves. Despite their pleas, the innocents were soon about to be hanged. As the story goes, Elijah Gossett, who had been a childhood friend of Crockett's in East Tennessee, lived nearby and happened along just in time to save Crockett's life. A less dramatic version of the story about the chance meeting of old friends says that Crockett rode past a public building that was under construction and recognized Gossett working there. He stopped, and the two men talked. That night, Gossett, his son Andrew Edward, and some neighbors rode out to Crockett's campsite to visit. At Andrew Edward Gossett's suggestion, the town was subsequently named Crockett.

Crockett and his party continued southwest, crossing the Trinity River at Nathaniel Robbins's ferry. At some point beyond that, they apparently turned off the Old San Antonio Road and headed south through a swamp toward Washington on the bank of the Brazos River (see the next section on Washington-on-the-Brazos State Historic Site).

Washington-on-the-Brazos State Historic Site

Washington-on-the-Brazos State Historic Site is located in east-central Texas eight miles southwest of Navasota off TX 105 by way of FM (farm road) 1155. The displays at the visitor center superbly interpret the history of the birth of the Republic of Texas. The tour includes the reconstructed Independence Hall, which was unfinished at the time the delegates to the Constitutional Convention met there in March 1836 to issue a declaration of independence and then hurriedly fash-

ion a constitution. An adjacent monument was erected by schoolchildren from nearby Brenham in 1899, some 16 years in advance of the park's establishment. Visitors can walk down Ferry Street to the site where David Crockett crossed the Brazos River. Also at the historic site is the Star of the Republic Museum, which interprets the history of the Republic of Texas (1836-46) with excellent, insightful displays.

As David Crockett and his party of riders traveled toward San Antonio from Nacogdoches, they approached Washington, departing the Old San Antonio Road and passing about four miles through a swamp where the water was two feet deep in places.

Arriving opposite Washington, Crockett and his men crossed the Brazos River below its confluence with the Navasota River, using the ferry founded before 1822 at the La Bahia Road crossing by Andrew Robinson. In 1835, Robinson's son-in law, John Hall, operated the ferry. Hall had surveyed the land and laid out a town in 1833. In 1835, he bought out Robinson's interest in land and

Delegates convened at Independence Hall to declare independence for Texas on March 2, 1836. A replica stands at the site today.

established the Washington Town Company. His business partner, Dr. Asa Hoxey, named the town after his hometown of Washington, Georgia.

Crockett rode up the hill and into town along Ferry Street, where the men found lodging at a hotel run by John Lott. One account described the hotel as a "disgusting place," a "wretchedly made establishment" with a "rowdy set lounging about." Most of the patrons slept on the floor, due to a lack of beds. Crockett signed a note to Lott for the accommodations, to be paid by the government. The note was dated January 23. No interpretive signs at the historic site mention the location of Lott's hotel.

Crockett was no stranger to the residents of Texas. Three-quarters of the settlers in Texas in 1836 had come from the United States. In fact, they had poured into this region of Mexico at the rate of 1,000 per month during the early 1830s. Crockett was a national celebrity in the United States, and recent American emigrants were eager to see him.

One account says that Crockett stayed in the Washington area for several days and visited with the Swisher family. Writing years later, John Mitchell Swisher, age 17 at the time of the visit, told of returning from a hunting trip to discover Crockett at his home. He wrote that Crockett praised him for his fine kill and then helped him dress the deer. During his stay, Crockett entertained the former Tennessee family well into the night with his wilderness tales and outlandish descriptions. He also challenged the young Swisher to a shooting match, which the writer described as a draw.

Swisher wrote of Crockett this way: "At the time I saw Colonel Crockett, I judged him to be about forty years old [actually 49]. He was stout and muscular, about six feet in height, and weighing 180 to 200 pounds. He was of a florid complexion, with intelligent gray eyes. He had small side whiskers inclining to sandy. His countenance, although firm and determined, wore a pleasant and genial expression."

Contrary to what Crockett had expected, General Sam Houston was not at Washington. It was there that Crockett may have learned about the dysfunctional Texas government, which now had a governor who had dismissed the legislature, a legislature that had fired the governor and sworn in the lieutenant governor, and divided armies each following orders issued by one or the other of the competing governors. Only one matter was clear: the imminent attack on San Antonio by a massive Mexican army believed to be pushing north. In response, companies of men under the leadership of Jim Bowie, William Travis, and Phillip Dimitt were standing by for orders or were already on their way to San Antonio. With this information, Crockett and his men decided not to wait for General Houston.

Some historians have suggested that if Crockett did not ride to Texas just to fight for its independence, he rode there because he

The Star of the Republic Museum presents the history of Texas's fight for independence and its 10 years as a republic.

saw the fight as the key to his political future. Indeed, if Crockett hoped to be elected to the Constitutional Convention by the company of volunteers, he needed to reach San Antonio by February 1. He had eight days to cover 160 miles. Given that Crockett arrived in San Antonio days after the voting and in fact took over two weeks to cover the 285 miles from Nacogdoches, it appears that he was not trying to achieve political success through election to the Constitutional Convention by the volunteers garrisoned at San Antonio. He may have thought he was a shoo-in by the vote of those in San Augustine, or he may have expected the upcoming military defense of San Antonio to elevate his political profile in the hoped-for new republic.

Whatever his motivation, Crockett rode away from Washington headed for the Alamo (see the section on Bastrop, pages 216-18).

Bastrop

Bastrop is located in Bastrop County southeast of Austin. It lies along the Colorado River at the convergence of TX 21, TX 95, and TX 71. At the time David Crockett visited the community, it was known as Mina, in honor of a Mexican hero. The town's early history is presented on a historic marker at TX 71 and Loop 150. Bastrop State Park is about two miles east of town along TX 21. A historic marker at the park entrance commemorates the Lost Pines.

As David Crockett traveled southwest from Washington toward San Antonio, he rode through the area known as the Lost Pines. The expanse of loblolly pines—100 miles removed from the pine forests of East Texas—covered perhaps 70 square miles. The unique

Crockett rode through the Lost Pines, commemorated today at Bastrop State Park.

environment that supported the pines was created during the re-cession of the glaciers at the close of the last Ice Age.

Bastrop, platted in 1832 and renamed Mina in 1834, was a com-munity along the Old San Antonio Road where riders could cross the Colorado River at Puesta del Colorado. Crockett was relieved to reach the town amidst the Lost Pines. By some accounts, only one companion, B. Archer M. Thomas, accompanied him there. Crockett needed a gunsmith to repair one of his rifles. He found such a craftsman, Kentuckian John Berry, in town. Berry repaired the break at the breech by placing a silver strap over the barrel. Crockett was much pleased, declaring the rifle better than when it was new.

Between Mina and San Antonio lay about 100 miles of open prairie. Facing the prospect of being attacked by Comanches, Crockett may well have waited in the town for a few more riders to help form a party large enough to provide protection for them all. This may have contributed to his arriving in San Antonio after the February 1 election.

During the Runaway Scrape—the panicked retreat of Texans in the face of Santa Anna's advance after the fall of the Alamo—the town of Mina was completely destroyed by Mexicans and Indians. In December 1837, it was returned to its original name of Bastrop. (For more information, see the next section on San Antonio.)

San Antonio

San Antonio is in south-central Texas where I-35, I-37, and I-10 converge in Béxar County. The Alamo is the shrine of Texas liberty. This honored site is bounded by East Houston Street, East Crockett Street, Bonham Street, and Alamo Street in the center of town. The site is open daily; hours vary during the year. Hats are not allowed in the shrine (or church). Photographs are not allowed in the shrine or in the Long Barrack Museum. The Daughters of the Republic of Texas operate and maintain the Alamo without the benefit of any government money. They have done so since 1905.

New exhibits opened in the Long Barrack Museum in October 2005. The museum includes David Crockett artifacts that do not relate just to his experience at the Alamo: a lock of his hair, his tin box and hairbrush, a knife he used while bear hunting, and a rifle he owned (converted by a subsequent owner from a flintlock to a percussion cap). Crockett items displayed in the sacristy inside the shrine are a reproduction of John Gadsby Chapman's 1834 painting of Crockett (the original has been retired from exhibition), a beaded buckskin vest given Crockett by a tribe of East Tennessee Indians, a rifle (sawed off and converted to percussion by a subsequent owner) and accouterments presented to him in Nashville in 1822, two shot flasks, a kidney-style possibilities bag, and a powder horn. Also displayed is the only known firearm recovered from the scene of the massacre at the Alamo. It is a Jacob Dikert long rifle made of pearly maple. Also in the church, in a room adjacent to the sacristy where the women and children hid during the attack, are the following items: a law book of Crockett's presented to a friend in 1828, a legal document signed by Crockett in 1818, a log from the chimney corner of his home in Rutherford, Tennessee, and a copy of Sketches and Eccentricities of Colonel David Crockett of West Tennessee, published in London in 1834. This is the bogus biography originally published in 1833 as Life and Adventures of Colonel David Crockett of West Tennessee.

In the center of the Alamo plaza is the Cenotaph, a white marble monument commemorating the sacrifice of the heroes of the Alamo. The names of all the fallen are engraved around the monument. Relief sculptures on the east and west faces prominently feature depictions of the four commanders of the Alamo garrison—William Barret Travis, Jim Bowie, David Crockett, and James Butler Bonham. The inscription on the monument reads, "In memory of the heroes who sacrificed their lives at The Alamo, March 6, 1836 in the defense of Texas. They chose never to surrender nor retreat; these brave hearts with flags still proudly waving, perished in the flames of immortality that their high sacrifice might lead to the founding of this Texas. Erected by the state of Texas 1936 with funds appropriated by the federal government to commemorate 100 years of Texas Independence. Pompeo Coppini, sculptor."

The site at which General Cos surrendered San Antonio (known as Béxar at the time) on December 10, 1835, is commemorated by

> *a marker in La Villita, which is today a boutique shopping district. The monument is near the entrance to the Arneson River Theater along the Riverwalk at 418 Villita Street.*
>
> *The San Fernando Cathedral is on Main Street between Commerce and Market streets, across from Plaza de las Islas. In the left entrance is a sarcophagus holding ashes from the pyres on which were burned the bodies of the Alamo defenders. Originally buried in the Old San Fernando Church, the remains were re-entombed in 1938. Though it sits on the same site, the current cathedral is not the same structure—the original San Fernando de Béxar—from whose bell tower Santa Anna hung the red flag in 1836 signaling, "No quarter."*

What is now San Antonio began as a collection of communities established for military, religious, and civil purposes. All were settled along the San Antonio River. The collective community was known generally as Béxar.

The Misión San Antonio de Valero was begun in 1718 and moved to the current site in 1724. It served the Indian community. When the mission was closed by the Catholic Church in 1793 and secularized by the Spanish, the local Indians continued to cultivate the fields around it. The parishioners attended services at San Fernando de Béxar, whose cornerstone was laid in 1738. In the early 1800s, a cavalry unit known as a "flying company" from Alamo de Parras was stationed at the former mission site. The fortified barracks became known as "the Alamo" after the unit's hometown. The word *Alamo* means cottonwood.

Inspired by the American Revolution and the French Revolution, the Mexicans pursued their independence from Spain in 1810. In 1812, Mexican and American volunteers occupied the Alamo for six months. They were defeated in 1813 by an army in which Anto-

The Alamo shrine has been operated by the Daughters of the Republic of Texas since 1905.

nio López de Santa Anna was a young officer. Twenty-three years later, Santa Anna came to the Alamo knowing its defenses.

Mexico won its independence in 1821. It established several district states, but so few people lived in Texas (or Tejas, a Caddo word meaning allies) that it was combined with another district, Coahuila, for administration. To help protect its northern border against Comanche and Apache raids, Mexico invited colonists from the United States to cross the border and settle in Coahuila y Tejas. Stephen F. Austin was the first colonizer from the United States. The American colonizers enjoyed relative freedom, thanks to their remoteness from Mexico City. They relied on the Federal Constitution of 1824 to protect their rights. To own land, they became Mexican citizens and accepted the Catholic faith. With these concessions, they were offered extensive tracts of land. Unfortunately, so many Americans came to Coahuila y Tejas—some 30,000 by 1830—that Mexico decided to close its borders, believing that the influence of the former United States citizens was getting too strong.

In 1833, Santa Anna was elected president of Mexico as a Federalist who supported the constitution of 1824. However, in 1834, with the help of the military, large landowners, and the Catholic

Church, Santa Anna discarded the 10-year-old constitution and became a Centralist dictator. The colonists in Texas were outraged. David Crockett probably saw in this act a reflection of what he had railed against for years—that is, President Andrew Jackson putting himself, in Crockett's opinion, above the United States Constitution.

During the summer of 1835, Texans sent delegates to a meeting to discuss what actions they should take in the face of Santa Anna's changes to Mexican governance. The meeting was called "the Consultation." It created plans for raising an army and later created a provisional government consisting of a governor assisted by a General Council. Henry Smith was elected governor.

That same summer, Santa Anna sent his brother-in-law, General Martín Perfecto de Cos, to recover a cannon from the fortification at Gonzales, about 40 miles east of San Antonio. The Texas colonists resisted, waving a flag that challenged the Mexican army with the words, "Come and Take It." The shots fired at Gonzales on October 2, 1835, started the Texas Revolution. Indeed, Gonzales was called "the Lexington of Texas." Crockett most likely heard

The story of the Alamo is told in the Wall of History.

news of this conflict in November as he rode into Jackson, Tennessee, on the initial leg of his journey to Texas.

On November 7, the Consultation issued the Declaration of Causes, which called for the reinstatement of the Federal Constitution of 1824. By December, the colonists had defended Gonzales and were fighting in San Antonio. From December 5 to December 9, the Texas colonists and Tejano residents (Mexican nationals in Texas) fought house-to-house through La Villita in what was known as the Battle of Béxar. Their force of 350 was reinforced by 120 men of the New Orleans Greys. General Cos was forced to surrender on December 11. As a result, the Texans occupied the Alamo. News of this conflict probably greeted Crockett when he arrived in Nacogdoches.

During the fall of 1835, while Crockett was alternately heading toward San Antonio to fight in the revolution and enjoying a sportsman's hunt, the political circumstances in Texas were changing. By the time he arrived at the Alamo in February 1836, news

A detailed layout of the Alamo in 1836 is presented in bronze in Alamo Plaza.

was circulating that a large army of Mexican soldiers was amassing with the intention of marching north to retake the Alamo and put an end to the insurrection. General Santa Anna was at the army's head.

Crockett biographer James Atkins Shackford pointed out that the events of the battle at the Alamo were told by the few survivors—namely, women, slaves, and children who were released by the victorious Mexicans. He noted that the recorded accounts disagree on almost all points, thus leaving the facts of what transpired on March 6 uncertain. The details of the events leading up to the last stand at the Alamo, however, are corroborated by many accounts and can be retold with some accuracy.

At the time of the siege of the Alamo in 1836, the church was unfinished. It had no roof. The distinctive curved parapet so strongly identified with the Alamo today was not there during the battle. It was added in 1850 by the United States Army. The plaza in front of the church was surrounded by a wall, along which were barracks.

Crockett arrived at San Antonio sometime between February 5 and 10. The exhibit in the Long Barrack Museum says the date was February 8. Regardless of any uncertainty about when it occurred, Crockett's entrance into the town is well described. Crockett sent one of his party into the community of 2,000 to ask that the celebrated Jim Bowie come out and escort him into town. According to historian Manley Cobia, Crockett was camped along San Pedro Creek near the old cemetery. From there, Bowie rode with him into town quite conspicuously. One eyewitness account written a lifetime later said that Crockett wore a buckskin suit and a coonskin cap. Upon Crockett's arrival, one account declared that he was given a "goods box" to stand on so he could address the crowd. The details of this supposed speech are debated by historians. Whether he actually did speak or not, a party was most certainly thrown on the night of February 11 in Crockett's honor. It was well attended and lasted far into the night. But the mood of the evening was interrupted by news arriving from distant spies.

Reports had circulated for weeks about a large army under the command of Santa Anna advancing toward San Antonio. A messenger arrived at the party after midnight with news that spies had reported that an army of 13,000 had begun marching toward San Antonio three days earlier. Prior to this news, reports had described an army of 1,000 to 2,000 soldiers. The message was given to Jim Bowie, who called William Travis from the dance floor to read it. Travis had just been made acting commander, as Colonel James Clinton Neill had departed that day to tend to personal matters. Travis, age 26, was infatuated with the charms of one particular woman that evening and was reluctant to leave the dance floor. Bowie insisted. Taking leave of the maiden he described as the most beautiful woman in town, Travis invited Crockett to join him and

The Long Barrack Museum stands on Convento Courtyard.

Bowie in discussing the news with Antonio Menchaca. After reading the message, Travis deduced that an army of 13,000 would take two weeks to get to San Antonio, and that much time remained for preparations. He returned to the dance floor and continued courting his love interest until the party ended at seven in the morning on February 12.

Though Travis had been put in charge of the garrison by Colonel Neill, the volunteers preferred to elect their own leaders. Travis agreed to hold an election. Some of the volunteers approached Crockett and asked him to run for commander. Travis offered Crockett a command. He declined both offers, saying he wanted only to serve as a "high private." The volunteers then elected Jim Bowie as their commander. He celebrated by getting drunk and immediately releasing all the prisoners. When the town protested, Bowie marched some of his loyal troops, also drunk, into the main square, where they paraded about waving their guns. Travis subsequently wrote a letter to the deposed governor, Henry Smith, asking for reassignment or for regular soldiers. In earlier letters, he had warned of the advance of a massive Mexican army. The situation had become more desperate.

Crockett most likely became aware of the full extent of the political chaos in Texas only after he arrived in San Antonio. Provisional Governor Henry Smith had disbanded the General Council, which in turn had impeached him and sworn in Lieutenant Governor James Robinson as acting governor. The council had then dissolved and become an advisory committee to the acting governor until the Constitutional Convention could assemble in March. Crockett may have desired a seat as a delegate to this convention. He said as much in a letter to his daughter written from San Augustine. If he had been elected as a delegate by the citizens of San Augustine in the February 1 election, Crockett knew that he would have been called by late February to convene. He had been very clear about his destination. There was no doubt that Texans could find him in San Antonio. Crockett accepted this realization of spoiled plans. Pursuing the path of a good republican who believed the job ought to seek the man, he in fact had not campaigned in earnest for a seat as a delegate.

To exacerbate the political problems, the armed forces of Texas were split. Acting Governor Robinson and his advisory committee reiterated their support for an army of volunteers on an expedition to Matamoros, where they thought they could defeat the thinned Mexican army. In early January, one of the leaders of this expedition took supplies from the garrison at San Antonio. He also convinced 200 men to leave the defense of that community to join the expedition to Matamoros. This left San Antonio with only 104 defenders. The original expedition to Matamoros was sent by the General Council, which was criticized for its action by Governor Smith. It was the disagreement between Smith and the council over this issue that led to his adjourning the council and, in response, the council's vacating his governorship.

General Sam Houston was serving under the deposed governor, Henry Smith, who refused to relinquish his position. Houston rode after the Matamoros expedition intending to stop it. In fact, Houston had sent Jim Bowie to San Antonio with a message for Colonel Neill telling him to destroy the Alamo so it could not be used by the advancing Mexican army. Neill was then to bring his volunteers to join Houston farther east and north at Goliad. Travis and Neill, however, believed that San Antonio should be defended against any Mexican advance. After Neill left the garrison in his command, Travis continued to ignore the orders to destroy the Alamo. Finding his position as commander in chief impossible to execute, Houston asked Governor Smith to parole him. It was under those conditions that Houston attended the Constitutional Convention in Washington, Texas, which convened on March 1. He was reaffirmed as commander in chief. It was also in Washington that Houston heard, on March 3, the plea from Colonel Travis for reinforcements to join him at San Antonio.

Protecting San Antonio had been the key to the Mexicans' failed strategy for defending the area a few months earlier. Now, with the vanquished armies of Mexico reappearing, it was time for the Texans to defend their homeland by protecting San Antonio. Even though the number of defenders was small, it was generally believed among the ranks that Texas militia would soon arrive to aid the defense. It was this faith, in part, that led Travis to disobey Houston's order to destroy the Alamo and retreat.

Meanwhile, the largest army that could aid the volunteers at San Antonio was under the command of Colonel James W. Fannin, who regarded himself as incompetent. He asked the acting governor to relieve him of command. Though some of the details of the situation were probably unknown to the men at San Antonio, it was clear to them that Travis's several requests for reinforcements had not been met. They were destined to face the advancing Mexican army alone, though they continued to hold out hope that the citizens of Texas would rally to their aid in defending the Alamo.

On the morning of February 23, the citizens were unprepared for what was approaching them from the south. The Dolores Cavalry of Santa Anna's army was riding toward San Antonio from its camp just eight miles away. Santa Anna and his army had arrived at the Medina River three days earlier but had been forced to wait for the river to recede before fording. He sent the cavalry ahead in part to secure a surrender. From the bell tower of the Old San Fernando Church, a lookout sent an alarm. Some men, including John Sutherland, rode out of town to see for themselves, then came back hurriedly. Sutherland met Crockett in the main plaza. The two went immediately to the Alamo to see Travis. According to Sutherland, Crockett said, "Colonel, here I am. Assign me a position, and I and my twelve boys will try to defend it." Travis told Crockett and his men to defend the "picket wall extending from the end of the barracks, on the south side, to the corner of the Church." As one faces the Alamo shrine today, this area is immediately in front of and to the right of the building.

Facing no resistance at all, the Mexican army advanced into San Antonio. As many of the residents abandoned the village, the volunteers retreated into the Alamo, which they had intended all along to use as their fortification. The Mexican army raised a red flag on the tower at the Old San Fernando Church, which signaled their intent to give no quarter—that is, to take no prisoners. In defiant response, Travis ordered his men to fire a cannon. Not satisfied that the other man was actually in charge, Travis and Bowie each sent separate messengers to talk with the Mexican army. Each returned with the same story—the defenders must surrender without conditions or die fighting.

Inside the fort, Jim Bowie, the elected leader of the volunteers, fell ill. Some accounts say he had pneumonia, while others say typhoid. Because his condition was feared initially to be contagious, Bowie was moved to separate quarters in the Low Barrack, where he was tended by one of the women in the fort, Madam Candelaria. Travis then took charge of the garrison.

The accounts of the fighting in the first few days differ. The Mexican army fired its artillery at the Alamo, bombarding the inhabitants throughout the day. Other accounts say that the Mexicans advanced toward the south wall, where they were repulsed after suffering casualties in an intense skirmish. One story relates that before the fighting actually began, Crockett picked off a Mexican

200 yards away, thanks to an extra charge of powder and superb marksmanship.

On February 25, the Mexican army attacked twice but was repulsed. Travis's report said, in part, "Today at 10:00 o'clock A.M. some two or three hundred Mexicans crossed the river below, and came up under the cover of the houses, until they arrived within point blank shot, when we opened a heavy discharge of grape and canister on them, together with a well directed fire from small arms, which forced them to halt and take shelter in the houses about 90 or 100 yards from our batteries. The action continued to rage for about two hours, when the enemy retreated in confusion, dragging off some of their dead or wounded." Travis praised the bravery of his men, including Crockett: "The Hon. David Crockett was seen at all points, animating the men to do their duty."

During the siege, Crockett made an effort to keep the fear of the moment from spreading. "Senor Crockett seemed everywhere," Enrique Esparza wrote of his experience then as a child. "He would shoot from the wall or through the portholes. Then he would run back and say something funny. He tried to speak Spanish sometimes. Now and then he would run to the fire we had in the courtyard where we were to make us laugh."

Crockett understood soldiers and frontiersmen. He knew when to fight and when to entertain. To help break the tension, he told the volunteers and the citizens inside the Alamo hunting stories and tales from his days in Congress. He had a fiddle as well, by some accounts, and though not very accomplished with it, he teamed with a bagpiper in making a raucous noise that helped the fighters forget for a moment the desperation of their plight.

Jacales—rude structures built of pickets and thatch—were within 100 yards or so to the south of the Alamo. On February 25, they provided cover for the Mexican army to advance within shooting range. To thwart the ease of another such advance, some of the men—Crockett is believed to have been one—stole from the safety of the Alamo that night to burn the rough buildings.

Water for the Alamo was supplied by an *acequia*, an irrigation ditch flowing from the San Antonio River. Knowing that the Mexicans could divert this water supply as part of their siege tactics, the defenders began to dig a well within the fortified area.

On February 26, a cold front arrived, bringing rain. Colonel Fannin at Fort Defiance in Goliad had been ordered to march 320 reinforcements to San Antonio to support the volunteers. Many of the soldiers considered it a suicide mission in the face of such a large Mexican army. Though Fannin escaped being caught in the open by the Mexican cavalry sent to destroy the advancing reinforcements, some say his cowardice and incompetence overtook him. While proceeding halfheartedly toward San Antonio, Fannin decided to turn around and march his men back to the safety of Fort Defiance.

On February 27, parties of men left the Alamo to forage for food. Accounts say they returned with 30 bushels of corn and some cattle. No one knew how long the siege would last. Mexican artillery continued to fire on the Alamo on February 28. The following day, leap-year day, was quiet. A truce may have been called by the Mexicans.

At three o'clock (some accounts say 11 o'clock) on the morning of March 1, a party of reinforcements rode into the Alamo, to the delight of the volunteers. They arrived "unmolested," wrote Travis, because the Dolores Cavalry was away. These reinforcements were the Gonzales Mounted Rangers, numbering 32 (some accounts say 37). Though this was the only documented arrival of reinforcements to the Alamo, author Manley Cobia, Jr., made a strong case for the possibility that other volunteers arrived in the company of Crockett, who had left the Alamo to recruit them.

Fragments of information from several accounts suggest the possibility that Crockett left the Alamo in the last days of February to meet volunteers arriving at Cibolo Creek Crossing, located 50 miles southeast of the Alamo, north of what is now Karnes City in Karnes County. The Texas Independence Trail crosses Cibolo Creek on TX 81 between Panna Maria and Helena. The riders met by Crockett may have been another portion of the Gonzales Mounted Rangers. Indeed, James Butler Bonham, one of the four commanders of the garrison, left the Alamo and rode to the community of Gonzales seeking reinforcements. He returned to the Alamo on March 3 with a letter to Travis from Major Robert Williamson, who declared that 60 men from Gonzales were on their way and that another 600 men were expected to convene shortly for a march to San Antonio. These mounted rangers and others began gathering at the crossing on February 28 awaiting the arrival of reinforcements from Goliad under Colonel Fannin, who they did not know had already turned around. If Crockett did meet the mounted rangers, he returned with some or all of them to the Alamo on March 3. By that time, the siege of the Alamo had strengthened, and the reinforcements, presumably including Crockett, had to fight their way back inside. Indeed, the *Arkansas Gazette* reported in April that "Col. Crockett, with about 50 resolute volunteers, had cut their way into the garrison, through the Mexican troops, only a few days before the fall of San Antonio." Mexican accounts offered confirmation of this arrival, though they mistakenly claimed the riders originated inside the Alamo.

Travis knew the circumstances were dire. He was gravely disappointed that only a small fraction of the reinforcements he had requested had arrived. On March 3, in his last message, he wrote, "I am determined to perish in the defense of this place, and may my bones reproach my country for her neglect."

On March 4, Travis and his garrison watched the cannons move closer to the Alamo as Santa Anna tightened his siege. On March 5, while Santa Anna was deciding to attack the Alamo the next day, Travis reportedly offered his fellow defenders a chance to leave. The popular account says that he drew a line in the dirt and asked all who were willing to stay and fight to step across. Tradition says all but one did.

Another popular story says that, probably on March 5, Crockett attempted another long-distance shot when Santa Anna rode toward the front to observe. He supposedly barely missed the dictator, who, perhaps in response, called for an all-out attack to begin in the morning.

Detailed plans were distributed to the Mexican officers. They called for attacks on four fronts by separate columns equipped with ladders, crowbars, and axes. Santa Anna had decided not to wait for the arrival of two 12-pound cannons he could have used to knock holes in the fortress walls. Instead, he elected to go over the walls, which were only eight to 12 feet high. Though he had by some accounts almost 2,600 men, Santa Anna used only those troops who were experienced; the new recruits remained back. The attack was to begin with the sound of a bugle at four in the morning. Accordingly, Santa Anna ceased his artillery barrage of the Alamo so his men could rest.

Before dawn on Sunday, March 6, the Alamo was attacked by 1,800 Mexican soldiers, according to some. The element of surprise was lost when one excited company sent up a cheer for Santa Anna. The Alamo garrison was asleep and not expecting to be attacked. The men had worked into the night strengthening their defenses and had retired late. When the charge began, one of the garrison aroused Travis from his sleep. Travis ran to his position on the north wall with his double-barreled shotgun. He leaned over the wall, fired once, and was immediately struck by return fire. He fell back dead. The Alamo had lost its commander almost instantly.

Two unsuccessful forays against the north wall were followed by a third. The Mexican reserves advanced and began to climb the walls using ladders. The Texans' cannons could not be pointed downward and so became useless after the attackers got close. But once the Mexicans commanded the walls and commandeered the cannons, they turned them on the Alamo church and began to blast at it with the fort's own artillery.

On the south side, Crockett's men repulsed an attack by 100 soldiers who later succeeded in coming over the southwest wall. Some of the volunteers, forced outside the compound and either hoping to escape or trying to gain an advantage by fighting in the open, were run down by the cavalry and killed.

As the Mexicans came over the walls, the fighting was fierce and confused. Over 500 Mexicans were killed, many of them shot by their own troops advancing behind them and firing into the dark. Soldiers found Jim Bowie in the Low Barrack under the care of Madam Candelaria. They killed him in his bed. The Mexican soldiers stormed the church, where the noncombatants had taken refuge. The church also housed one of the gun placements and a store of powder. The Texas artillerymen attempted to ignite the powder to destroy it but were killed before they could. For the others remaining elsewhere inside the compound, the Long Barrack became their final fortress as they retreated there for their last stand. The slaughter was nearly complete. The killing was finished before sunrise. The noncombatants—women, children, and slaves—were spared. Some accounts say five or seven men from the garrison were captured.

By all accounts, every member of the Alamo garrison was killed. In his own translated journal, Santa Anna recorded his orders to the authorities in San Antonio to account for and identify three specific bodies: "Among the dead are the first and second enemy commanders, Bowie and Travis. Colonels they were. Of the same rank was Crockett." Santa Anna then ordered that funeral pyres be built. The bodies were laid between layers of wood and set afire. The pyres burned on each side of the road leading east, Calle del Portero (now Commerce Street). At the time, this road, lined with cottonwood trees, was also called the Alameda. By the end of the day on which the Alamo fell, the volunteers had completely disappeared, their bodies consumed by flames.

On March 11, General Sam Houston sent orders to Colonel Fannin at Goliad. Relating the events at San Antonio as he understood them at the time, he wrote, "The Alamo was attacked on Sunday morning at dawn of day, by about 2,300 Mexicans and was carried a short time before sunrise, with a loss of 520 Mexicans killed and as many wounded. Col. Travis had only 150 effective men out of his whole force of 187. After the fort was carried, seven men surrendered and called for Gen. Santa Anna for quarter—they were murdered by his orders. Col. Bowie, was sick in bed, and also murdered." Biographer James Shackford corrected this account, accepting 5,000 as the size of the Mexican army, with 1,544 dead.

Exactly how Crockett died is a matter of speculation and contested documentation. On March 20, Joe, a black slave of William Travis and a survivor of the massacre, reported that "Crockett and a few of his friends were found together, with twenty-four of the enemy dead around them." A few days later, the citizens of Nacogdoches proclaimed within a resolution, "David Crockett (now rendered immortal in Glory) had fortified himself with sixteen

Above: *The* Cenotaph *at Alamo Plaza
commemorates the martyrs of the Alamo
massacre.*
Right: *David Crockett is portrayed on the*
Cenotaph *as one of the four Alamo
commanders.*

guns well charged, and a monument of slain foes encompasses his lifeless body."

During the month of March and afterward, newspapers recanted their earlier reports that Crockett had died on the frontier, possibly at the hands of Comanches. They boasted instead of the success of the Alamo's volunteers in repulsing the Mexican attacks of February 25. The facts were wildly exaggerated. The stories told of

500 Mexicans dead without the loss of a single Texan. But soon enough, the news of the fall of the Alamo reached the newspapers, primarily through reports from New Orleans.

On April 7, one letter to a newspaper said, "The Hon. David Crockett is no more." It continued, "After the massacre he was found with the breech of his gun broke off, and it grasped by the muzzle in his left hand, and his butcher knife in his right. Both told a tale of death—for they were bathed in the blood of his enemies."

These accounts gave rise to the popular image of Crockett heroically fighting to the death at the Alamo, engaged in hand-to-hand combat and suffering a soldier's noble fate. Not surprisingly, later alternate accounts were greeted with derision by those schooled on the traditional story. The alternate accounts told of a less dramatic, though no less heroic, end for Crockett.

Some of the earliest stories about the fall of the Alamo included Crockett as one of the men captured alive. As a prisoner, he supposedly lunged at the throat of Santa Anna and was killed only inches from strangling the hated dictator. Those who preferred to see Crockett as courageously fighting to the death while swinging Old Betsy disputed that tale, favoring what became the traditional account.

With Santa Anna in Texas: A Personal Narrative of the Revolution by Jose Enrique de la Peña offered another account of Crockett's death at the Alamo. Said to be a translated diary, it provided source material for Alamo scholars from a Mexican perspective. The account reported "naturalist David Crockett, very well known in North America for his strange adventures," as one of seven persons taken prisoner. (Though Sam Houston's contemporary account acknowledged the taking and subsequent murder of prisoners, Crockett was not confirmed to be among them. Moreover, other accounts told of five, not seven, men captured.) The prisoners were presented to Santa Anna, who, said some, was angered that his policy of not giving quarter had been violated. He ordered the prisoners executed immediately. According to de la Peña, it was ordered with a simple dismissive gesture and with no display of anger at the officer who brought them forward. Some said the soldiers under General Manuel Fernandez Castrillón, who had captured the men, resisted the order and that members of Santa Anna's personal guard, standing nearby, then drew their swords. In the words of de la Peña, the Mexicans "fell upon these unfortunate, defenseless men just as a tiger leaps upon his prey. Though tortured before they were killed, these unfortunates died without complaining and without humiliating themselves before their torturers." The Mexican officers ran the prisoners through. None begged for mercy; all died with dignity.

Some historians have contested this account, saying that the non-English-speaking de la Pena may have confused the Anglo names Crockett and Cochran when writing his account. Moreover, subsequent research of the source document has called its authenticity into question. Though originally called a diary, it is now regarded as a memoir to which some material was added later from historical records. Nevertheless, at the time of its translation in 1975 and through subsequent promotion in a short volume called *How Did Davy Die?* by Dan Kilgore, this translation was used by some to impugn Crockett's heroism. Others, clinging to the traditional view of Crockett's death, lambasted the translator for suggesting that Crockett surrendered. For those who hold dear to the image of defiant Texans fighting to the death in defense of the Alamo, the word *surrender* suggests some degree of cowardice. Archivist and translator Carmen Perry reminded historians that the words *surrender* and *capture* did not appear in the de la Peña papers, and that she had only translated what others had written.

In April 2000, the Center for American History at the University of Texas held a one-day conference to discuss the narrative of Jose Enrique de la Peña. After the Texas Revolution ended, de la Peña expanded his diary into a memoir of the events of December 1835 through April 1836. A documentary movie entitled *Davy Crockett and the de la Peña Diary* was shown at the conference. It explored the claims of those who accepted the document's authenticity and those who claimed it to be a forgery. Historians remain divided.

Though the details of Crockett's death remain unresolved, it is apparent that he died while engaged in a heroic struggle against vastly superior numbers. His presence at the Alamo alone has warranted his celebration even today as a hero of the common man. His death there, regardless of the circumstances, greatly inspired the Texas armies, which decisively prevailed in the revolution that ended just seven weeks later at San Jacinto in an attack prosecuted by Crockett's fellow Tennessean Sam Houston.

Madam Candelaria, who tended the ailing Jim Bowie, was interviewed 52 years after the Alamo massacre. From her account, which Shackford accepted as reliable, the interviewer wrote, "Returning to the subject of David Crockett, the old Senora said he was one of the first to die; that he had advanced from the Church building towards the rampart running from the end of the stockade, slowly and with great deliberation, without arms, when suddenly a volley was fired by the Mexicans causing him to fall forward on his face, dead."

Another eyewitness account by Mrs. Susanna Dickerson (or Dickenson) said, "As we passed through the enclosed ground in front of the Church, I saw heaps of dead and dying. . . . I recognized Col. Crockett lying dead and mutilated between the church and the two story barrack building, and even remember seeing his peculiar cap lying by his side." Shackford noted that Mrs. Dickerson's

Ashes of the fallen heroes are kept at the San Fernando Cathedral.

several accounts were occasionally self-contradictory and that she was inside the church during the last stand, unable to observe events firsthand. Moreover, she was greatly distressed at the loss of her husband and young son in the fight.

News of the defeat at the Alamo traveled slowly east. It was a month before the residents of Little Rock heard and weeks more before the citizens of the United States farther east learned of the fate of the brave volunteers. The Crockett family may well have learned of their husband's and father's death from Dr. Isaac N. Jones of Lost Prairie, Arkansas. He returned to Elizabeth Crockett a letter, along with the watch Crockett had traded him for his own watch and $30 while Crockett was on his way to Nacogdoches. Shortly after that, Crockett's son John Wesley wrote a letter to his mother's family in North Carolina telling of Crockett's death in Texas.

John Wesley Crockett was elected to a seat in Congress in 1837. During his second term, Congress passed a law allowing the residents of West Tennessee to purchase land from the state at 12 and a half cents per acre. David Crockett's legislative ambition was finally realized.

In 1840, an American returning from Mexico related that he had spoken with a man there who claimed to be David Crockett. John Wesley Crockett heard and desperately wanted to believe the rumor that his father had been taken prisoner and was a forced laborer in a mine in Guadalajara. Using his position as a congressman, he pursued the matter through the secretary of state. After an investigation, the American minister to Mexico reported that the subject prisoner had died.

As the story of the Alamo was absorbed across America in 1836, a patriotic fervor was ignited. David Crockett had been an eccentric character—a wild man of the West to some, a buffoon to others, but always a friend and champion to the poor, powerless settlers who were continually moving westward in search of land and opportunity. He was a nationally known figure and a symbol of America's passion for independence and self-sufficiency. His passing, especially at the hands of an enemy run by a dictator, caused an outpouring of support for helping Texas secure its freedom. As a celebrated martyr in the pursuit of Texas freedom, Crockett surpassed all the expectations of fame he ever harbored.

David Crockett died in his 50th year without ever achieving the wealth and social standing that had so long eluded him. But through his celebrity and his martyred death, he was raised high as an American frontier folk hero. He was, at the end of his life, finally and truly borne to a mountain top.

APPENDIX
David Crockett Sites in Chronological Order

This appendix will prove useful to those who wish to read the episodes of Crockett's life in the order in which he lived them.

1777	Rogersville, Tennessee
1786-94	Davy Crockett Birthplace State Park, Tennessee
c. 1794-1805	Morristown, Tennessee
c. 1798	Natural Bridge, Virginia
c. 1799	Cheek's Crossroads, Tennessee
c. 1800	Gerrardstown, West Virginia
	Baltimore, Maryland
c. 1801	Radford, Virginia
1805-11	Dandridge, Tennessee
1811-13	Lynchburg, Tennessee
1813-17	Maxwell, Tennessee
1813	Winchester, Tennessee
	Huntsville, Alabama
	Tuscaloosa, Alabama
	Ohatchee, Alabama
	Tallasehatchee, Alabama
	Talladega, Alabama
1814	Fort Mims, Alabama
	Pensacola, Florida
	Sylacauga, Alabama

1816	Swannanoa, North Carolina
	Fairview, North Carolina
1817	David Crockett State Park, Tennessee
1817-21	Lawrenceburg, Tennessee
1821	Murfreesboro, Tennessee
1821-35	Rutherford, Tennessee
1821	Centerville, Tennessee
1825	Reelfoot Lake State Park, Tennessee
1826	Memphis, Tennessee
1827	Pleasant Gardens, North Carolina
	Tuxedo, North Carolina
	Trenton, Tennessee
1827-35	Washington, District of Columbia
1833	Jackson, Tennessee
1834	Philadelphia, Pennsylvania
1835	Little Rock, Arkansas
	Washington, Arkansas
	Jonesboro Crossing, Texas
	Clarksville, Texas
	Honey Grove, Texas
	De Kalb, Texas
1836	Nacogdoches, Texas
	San Augustine, Texas
	Crockett, Texas
	Washington-on-the-Brazos State Historic Site, Texas
	Bastrop, Texas
	San Antonio, Texas
1853	Acton, Texas
Present	Knoxville, Tennessee

Bibliography

Burstein, Andrew. *The Passions of Andrew Jackson*. New York: Alfred A. Knopf, 2003.

Cobia, Manley F., Jr. *Journey into the Land of Trials*. Franklin, TN: Hillsboro Press, Providence Publishing Corp., 2003.

Crockett, David. *A Narrative of the Life of David Crockett of the State of Tennessee*. 1834. Reprint, Lincoln, NE, and London: University of Nebraska Press, 1987.

Derr, Mark. *The Frontiersman: The Real Life and the Many Legends of Davy Crockett*. New York: William Morrow and Company, 1993.

Dooley, Claude W., and Betty Dooley Aubrey. *Why Stop? A Guide to Texas Historical Roadside Markers*. 3rd ed. Houston, TX: Gulf Publishing Company, 1992.

Forester, Cathy Tudor, ed. *Tennessee Historical Markers*. 8th ed. Nashville, TN: Tennessee Historical Commission, 1996.

Foster, Dave. *Franklin: The Stillborn State and the Sevier / Tipton Political Feud*. 2nd ed. Johnson City, TN: Overmountain Press, 2003.

Groneman, William, III. *David Crockett: Hero of the Common Man*. New York: Tom Daugherty Associates, LLC, 2005.

Handbook of Texas Online. 2005. http://www.tsha.utexas.edu/handbook/online.html. October 2005.

Hill, Michael R. *The Carson House of Marion, North Carolina*. Marion, NC: Historic Carson House, Inc., 2004.

Hood, Hugh M., Jack B. Hood, Sara M. Hood, and Laura C. Hood. *Alabama Historical Association Markers*. Birmingham, AL: Brookside Publishing, 2001.

Lofaro, Michael A., ed. *Davy Crockett: The Man, the Legend, the Legacy, 1786-1986*. Knoxville, TN: University of Tennessee Press, 1985.

Parris, Joyce Justus. *A History of Black Mountain North Carolina and Its People*. Black Mountain, NC: Black Mountain Centennial Commission, Swannanoa Valley Museum, 1992.

Remini, Robert V. *Andrew Jackson and the Course of American Empire*. New York: Harper & Row, 1977.

Sakowski, Carolyn. *Touring the East Tennessee Backroads*. Winston-Salem, NC: John F. Blair, Publisher, 1993.

Shackford, James Atkins. *David Crockett: The Man and the Legend*. 1956. Reprint, Lincoln, NE, and London: University of Nebraska Press, 1994.

Sondley, Foster A. *A History of Buncombe County, North Carolina*. Asheville, NC: The Advocate Printing Company, 1930.

Tessier, Mitzi Schaden. *The State of Buncombe*. Virginia Beach, VA: The Donning Company, 1992.

Winders, Richard Bruce. *Sacrificed at the Alamo: Tragedy and Triumph in the Texas Revolution*. Abilene, TX: State House Press, 2004.

Index

Abingdon, VA, 11,140
Abingdon-Knoxville Road, 11, 15, 150
Acton, TX, 201
Adams, John Quincy, 59, 77, 158, 168
Adeline (slave), 79
Alabama Cutoff, 127, 128, 129
Alabama River, 39, 42
Alameda, 235
Alamo de Parras, 220
Alamo, the, 52, 136, 167, 216, 218, 223-41
Alexander, Adam, 63, 76, 84
Apalachicola River, 113, 130, 133
Arkansas Advocate, 189
Arkansas Gazette, 81, 160, 187, 189, 232
Articles of Confederation, 3
Asheville, NC, 140, 145, 147
Austin, Stephen F., 195, 221

Baltimore, MD, 11, 12, 13, 40, 152, 156, 170-79, 181
Barnum's City Hotel, 175
Bastrop, TX, 216-18
Bean's Creek, 38, 40, 41-46, 48, 105, 115, 119, 127, 139
Beasley, Daniel, 124-26
Beaty, Robert, 96
Beaty's Spring, 40, 96, 99
Bateman's Drops, 120
Barnum, David, 175
Becknell, William, 195, 196, 198
Bedford, VA, 12
Bell Tavern, 88
Bent Creek Baptist Church, 14
Berry, John, 217

Béxar. *See* San Antonio, TX
Béxar, Battle of, 223
Biddle, Nicholas, 20, 161, 164, 166, 168
Birmingham, AL, 118
Black, James, 186, 190
Black Mountain, 144
Black Warrior River, 46, 48, 100, 117, 118, 119, 127
Black Warrior Town, 100, 116, 117, 119, 122
Blackhawk. *See* Huntsman, Adam
Blevins, Armstead, 191
Blount, Willie, 108
Blountville, TN, 11
Blue, Uriah, 130, 132
Boiling Fork Creek, 39
Bois d'Arc Creek, 198
Bolivar, TN, 92
Bonham, James Butler, 232
Boone, Daniel, 9, 42, 196
Boone, Daniel Morgan, 196
Boston, MA, 177
Bowie, Jim, 210, 215, 224, 225, 226, 227, 229, 234, 235, 239
Brahan, John, 96
Brahan Springs, 95
Brazos River, 213
Bristol, TN, 11
Brown's Purchase, 5
Buncombe Turnpike, 140, 147
Burgin, Abner, 81, 206
Burgin, Alney, 146
Burke County, NC, 138, 143, 144, 145
Burnt Corn Creek, Battle of, 96, 123, 125
Butler, William E., 74-76

Caldwell, James, 152
Call, Richard, 108

Caller, James, 123
Camp Wills, 102, 118
Campbell (neighbor), 6
Canady, John. *See* Kennedy, John
Candelaria, Madam, 229, 234,
    239
Cannon, Newton, 39
Carey & Hart, 174, 178
Carroll County, TN, 33-34, 53,
    70, 79
Carroll, William, 33, 36, 50, 54,
    70
Carson, John, 135, 144, 145
Carson, Samuel Price, 134, 140,
    145-48, 158
Carson House, 134-36
Castrillón, Manuel Fernandez,
    238
Catala, Bob, 106
Catawba River, 138, 143, 144
Centerville, TN, 54-56
Chapman, John Gadsby, 167
Charleston Courier, 81
Charlottesville, VA, 12
Chattahoochee River, 133
Cheek, Jesse, 11, 16
Cheek's Crossroads, 11
Cherokees, 4, 8-10, 118, 160
Chesapeake Bay, 196
Chester Gap, VA, 12
Chestnut Street Theater, 183
Chickamaugas, 8
Chickasaws, 46, 48, 122, 130-33
Chilton, Thomas, 161, 174
Choctaw Bayou, 198
Choctaws, 122, 130-33, 190
Christiansburg, VA, 12, 152
"Chronicles," 59, 61
Cibolo Creek, 232
City Hotel, 92
Clark, Isabella, 195, 196, 197

Clark, James, 195
Clark, William, 168, 177
Clarke, Matthew St. Clair, 161
Clarksville, TX, 191, 195-200
Clay, Henry, 76, 77
Clayton, Augustin Smith, 178
Coahuila y Tejas, 221
Cobia, Manley F., Jr., 81, 92, 94,
    188, 191, 195, 198, 205, 207,
    224, 231
Cocke, John, 102
Coffee, John, 99, 100, 102, 105-
    9, 116, 118, 127
Cole (Virginia resident), 151
Colorado River, 217
Comanches, 196, 198, 199, 217,
    221, 236
Conecuh River, 132
Congressional Reservation Line,
    31, 34
Constitution of 1824 (Mexico),
    205, 221-22
Constitutional Convention, 136,
    207, 210, 216, 226, 228
Consultation, the, 222, 223
Cooper, Joe, 94
Coosa River, 98-99, 101, 102,
    111, 114
Cornwallis, Charles, 143
Cos, Martín Perfecto de, 222,
    223
Crawley, Martha, 117, 122
Creeks, 8, 39, 42, 95-99, 100-
    105, 105-9, 111, 121-28, 130
Crisp, Mansil, 54
Crockett, Aaron (brother), 6
Crockett Almanacs, 188
Crockett, David (grandfather), 5,
    10
Crockett, Elizabeth (sister), 6, 17
Crockett, Elizabeth Patton

(second wife), 36, 45, 49, 65, 80, 120, 138, 199, 201-2, 240
Crockett, James Patterson (brother), 6
Crockett, James (uncle), 9
Crockett, John (father), 2-7, 8-10, 11, 14-18, 19, 80, 143
Crockett, John Wesley (son), 34, 38, 65, 67-70, 240, 241
Crockett, John (brother), 6, 11-12, 114, 154
Crockett, Joseph (uncle), 9
Crockett, Margaret (daughter), 44, 210
Crockett, Mary "Polly" Finley (first wife), 27, 29, 37, 43, 44, 45, 48
Crockett, Matilda (daughter), 201
Crockett, Nathan (brother), 6
Crockett, Rebecca (sister), 6
Crockett, Rebecca Hawkins (mother), 2, 4-5, 14, 15
Crockett, Robert Patton, 84, 202
Crockett Tavern, 11, 13, 17, 19, 151
Crockett, TX, 211-12
Crockett, William (brother), 6
Crockett, William (son), 38
Crockett, William (uncle), 10

Dandridge, Martha, 21
Dandridge, TN, 20-27
David Crockett State Park, 47-50
David Crockett's Bridle Trail, 135, 140-42, 147
Davis, Warren C., 146
Davis, William D., 93, 94
Davy Crockett Birthplace State Park, 1-7
Debates. See Register of Debates in Congress

De Kalb, TX, 192-93, 199
de la Peña, Jose Enrique, 237, 238, 239
Declaration of Causes, 223
Declaration of Independence (TX), 212
Declaration of Independence (US), 182
Delaware City, 176
Delaware River, 176
Derr, Mark, 26, 161, 164
Dickens, Asbury, 164
Dickerson, Susanna, 239
Dimitt, Phillip, 215
Ditto's Landing, AL, 97-99, 117, 118, 119
Doggett, Thomas, 27
Dolores Cavalry, 228, 231
Donelson, Emily, 135
Downing Gazette, 60
Downing, Major Jack, 60, 176
Dragging Canoe, 8
du Pont de Nemours, E. I., 183
Duck River, 28, 54, 117, 122
Dunn (wagoner), 150-51

East Tennessee Historical Society, 28
El Camino Real, 193, 211
Elder, Margaret, 24
Elk Creek, 116
Elk River, 28, 37
Ellicott Mills, 172
Ellms, Charles, 188
Emuckfaw, Battle of, 105
Escambia River, 130-33
Esparza, Enrique, 230

Fairview, NC, 140-42
Fannin, James W., 228, 231, 232, 235

Fayetteville, AL, 112
Fayetteville, TN, 127
Fells Point, 172
Ferguson, Patrick, 4, 143, 144
Finley, Jean, 27
Finley, William, 27, 38
First Presbyterian Church
   (Murfreesboro, TN), 34
Fish Dams, 102
Fish House, 181
Fitzgerald, William, 59, 163, 165
Forbes, John J., 205, 208
Fort Barrancas, 128, 130
Fort Chiswell, VA, 11
Fort Decatur, 113, 114, 133
Fort Defiance, 231
Fort Deposit, 101
Fort Deposite. See Fort Deposit
Fort Mims, 39, 42, 96, 106, 121-
   28, 130
Fort Montgomery, 128, 130
Fort Strother, 101, 102, 106, 109,
   110, 112, 114, 115, 133
Fort Talladega. See Lashley's Fort
Fort Watauga, 2
Fort Williams, 114
Franklin, Benjamin, 2
Franklin County, TN, 38, 39-40,
   42, 48
Franklin, State of, 1-5, 30
Frazier (Bean's Creek neighbor),
   119
French Broad River, 140
French, James Strange, 161, 164
Front Royal, VA, 12
Fulton, AR, 191

Gadsden, AL, 118
Galbraith, Thomas, 14
Gerrardstown, WV, 12, 155-56,
   172

Gibson County, TN, 62, 76, 80,
   92, 96
Gibson, John H., 96, 97
Gilbert Town, 144
Giles County, TN, 48
Goliad, TX, 227, 231, 232, 235
Gonzales Mounted Rangers, 231,
   232
Gonzales, TX, 62, 222, 223, 232
Gossett, Andrew Edwards, 212
Gossett, Elijah, 212
Gray, John, 12
Greene County, TN, 5, 14
Greeneville, TN, 11, 12, 147
Griffith, Elijah, 152
Guadalajara, Mexico, 241

Hackett, James, 164, 165
Hall, John, 213
Halley's Comet, 82
Hamblen County, TN, 10
Hamilton County, TN, 32
Hammond, Captain, 106
Harris, Flavius, 70
Hart's Saloon, 93
Hawkins, Joseph, 7, 28
Hawkins, Sarah, 5
Hawkins County, TN, 8
Henry, Abram, 67, 69
Hermitage Inn, 182
Hermitage, The (TN), 108
Hickman County, TN, 53, 54-56
Hill, Elizabeth Cooper, 142
Hillsborough, NC, 3
Hinderliter Grog Shop, 187
Hobb's Island, 101
Holmes, Thomas, 126
Holm's Village, 133
Holston River, 2, 10, 19
Honey Grove, TX, 198, 200
Honeycomb Creek, 101

Horseshoe Bend, Battle of, 105
Houston, Sam, 135, 160, 189, 195, 206, 210, 227, 228, 237, 239
Hoxey, Asa, 214
Humbert, Samuel, 7, 28
Humbert, Sarah, 7
Humphreys County, TN, 122
Hunter, 183
Huntsman, Adam, 58, 59, 61, 81, 93
Huntsville, AL, 40, 96-99

Indian Removal Bill, 160

Jackson, Andrew, 35, 46, 48, 58, 59, 60, 77, 96, 99, 101-4, 106, 108, 109-12, 116, 123, 127, 128, 133, 135, 159, 160, 161, 162, 165, 166, 169, 176, 177, 181, 182, 187, 196, 205, 222
Jackson, Rachel, 108, 135
Jackson, TN, 56-62, 74, 92, 186, 199, 223
Jefferson County, TN, 15, 27, 37
Jeffries Hotel, 187
John Swift Silver Mines, 9
Jones, Devil John, 118
Jones, Francis, 39, 96
Jones, Henry, 194
Jones, Isaac Newton, 199, 240
Jones, Jesse, 120
Jones Valley, 119
Jonesboro Crossing, TX, 191, 194-95
Jonesborough, TN, 3, 11, 146

Kendall, Amos, 6
Kennedy, John, 18-20, 21, 24, 27, 29
Kentuck, 42, 196

Kilgore, Dan, 238
Kings Mountain, Battle of, 4, 143, 144
King's Road. *See* El Camino Real
Kitchen, Benjamin, 16
Knoxville, TN, 28-29

La Bahia Road, 213
La Villita, 223
Lancaster County, PA, 183
Lashley's Fort, 102, 110, 111, 114
Latimer, Betty, 196
Latimer, Jane, 196
Lawrence, Amos, 177
Lawrence County, AL, 116
Lawrence County, TN, 47-50, 51-54, 67, 70
Lawrenceburg, TN, 50, 51-54
Leslie's Fort. *See* Lashley's Fort
Limestone Creek, 2, 6
Lincoln County, NC, 5
Lincoln County, TN, 38, 42
Lincoyer (Lyncoya), 108
Lion of the West, The, 161, 164, 175
Little Rock, AR, 94, 185-89, 240
Little Warrior, 117,122
Logansport, LA, 200
Long Island Treaty, 8
Lost Pines, 216, 217
Lost Prairie, AR, 199, 200, 240
Lott, John, 214
Lowell, MA, 177
Lynchburg, TN, 37-38
Lynchburg, VA, 12

Madison, VA, 12
Madison County, AL, 95
Madison County, TN, 56-61, 74
Marion, AR, 186

Marion, VA, 11
Matamoros, Mexico, 227
Matthews, Captain, 52
Matthews, Mansil W., 199
Maxwell, TN, 41-46
Mayo, Frank, 26
McBrayer, Samuel, 142
McCool (tavern keeper), 93
McDaniel (Obion R. neighbor),
    85-87
McDowell, Charles, 143, 144
McDowell, Joseph, 135
McDowell, Mary Moffitt, 135
McDowell, Silas, 145, 147
McIntosh, William, 122
McKinney, Colin, 199
McLemore's Bluff, 68, 70
McMinn County, TN, 32
McQueen, Peter, 96, 122
Meagher, Paddy, 89
Medina River, 228
Melton Bluff, 116, 127
Memphis, TN, 87-94
Menchaca, Antonio, 226
Miller County, AR, 195
Mill's Point, TN, 184
Mims, Samuel, 123
Mina. See Bastrop, TX
Misión San Antonio de Valero,
    220
Mississippi River, 78, 84, 88-92,
    186, 199
Mississippi State Convention, 59
Mitchell, James C., 32-33
Mobile, AL, 114, 124, 127, 128
Montgomery County, VA, 152,
    153
Monument Square, 175
Moore, Lieutenant, 106
Moore County, TN, 38
Morganton, NC, 4, 145, 147

Morristown, TN, 13-20
Mossy Creek, 15
Mulberry Fork of the Black
    Warrior River, 116
Mulberry Fork of the Elk River,
    38, 42, 48
Murfreesboro, TN, 29-37, 49, 50,
    52, 53
Murfreesborough. See
    Murfreesboro, TN
Muscle Shoals, AL, 116, 127
Musgokees (Creeks), 122
Myers, Adam, 12-13, 152, 156,
    172, 173-74
Myers, Henry, 173-74

Nacogdoches, TX, 193, 197, 199,
    200, 202-8, 210, 211, 213,
    216, 223, 235, 240
Nashville, TN, 40, 188
Natchez, MS, 92, 124
Natchitoches, LA, 191
National Banner and Nashville Whig,
    162
Natural Bridge, VA, 15, 149-51
Navasota River, 213
Neill, James Clinton, 225, 226,
    227
New Glasgow, VA, 12
New London, VA, 12
New Madrid earthquake, 67
New Orleans, LA, 78, 89, 127,
    128, 132, 237
New Orleans Greys, 203, 223
New River, 153
New York City, NY, 60, 177
Nichols, James, 191
Nile's Weekly Register, 204
Nimrod Wildfire. See Wildfire,
    Colonel Nimrod
Nolichucky River, 1-6, 14

Oath of Allegiance, 205, 206
Obion Lake, 78
Obion River, 34, 36, 50, 54, 67-70, 71, 77, 78, 79
Ohio River, 48, 183
Ohatchee, AL, 100
Oklahoma, 160, 191, 195
Old Brick Springs, 209
Old San Antonio Road, 209, 211, 212, 213, 217
Old Southwest Trail, 190, 191, 193
Old Stone Fort, 205, 208
Opequon River, 156
Orange Court House, VA, 12
Overmountain Men, 4
Overton, John, 77
Owens (neighbors), 67-70

Paddy's Hen-and-Chicks, 89
Panther Creek, 19
Panther Springs Academy, 13
Paris, TN, 163
Paris, TX, 197
Patton, Elijah, 138
Patton, George, 79
Patton, James, 138-39
Patton, Robert, 30, 67, 79, 81, 138, 143, 144
Patton, William, 81, 206
Paulding, James Kirke, 164
Pensacola, FL, 123, 127, 128, 129-30, 132
Perry, Carmen, 238
Philadelphia, PA, 80, 167, 176, 178, 180-84
Pleasant Gardens, NC, 134-36, 146-47
Potomac River, 156
Providence, RI, 177, 178

Radcliff (settler in Creek Nation), 97-98, 101
Radford, VA, 12, 153
Rattlesnake Branch, 38, 42
Red Eagle, 96, 109, 121-27
Red Mountain, 119
Red River, 136, 191, 194, 195, 199
Red Sticks, 96, 110, 111, 112, 114, 122, 123, 127, 128, 130-33
Reelfoot Lake State Park, 83-87
Reems Creek, 144
Registers of Debates in Congress, 159, 160
Rhea County, TN, 32
Rich (Bean's Creek neighbor), 119, 120
Robbins, Nathaniel, 212
Roberts, Elijah, 210
Robinson (Beans' Creek neighbor), 119, 120
Robinson, Andrew, 213
Robinson, James, 226, 227
Rock Mountain, 119
Rockbridge County, VA, 15, 150
Rogersville, TN, 8
Rucker's Creek, 201
Runaway Scrape, 218
Rusk, Thomas Jefferson, 206
Russell, George, 96-97
Russell, William, Jr., 113
Russell, William, Sr., 39, 96, 111, 113, 114, 127, 130-33
Rutherford, Griffith, 144
Rutherford, TN, 65-82, 92
Rutherford Fork of the Obion River, 50, 66, 84

Sabine River, 196, 200

Salem, VA, 12
Salem, TN, 40
Saluda Gap, 146
San Antonio, TX, 189, 192, 197, 213, 215, 216, 217, 218-41
San Augustine, TX, 205, 209-10, 226
San Fernando de Béxar, 220, 228
San Jacinto, 279
San Pedro Creek, 224
Santa Anna, Antonio López de, 205, 218, 221, 222, 224, 225, 233, 235, 237, 238
Santa Fe Trail, 196
Schuylkill River, 181
Scotland, 184
Second United States Bank, 36, 57, 104, 161, 164, 165, 176
Separate Battalion of Tennessee Mounted Gunmen, 127
Sevier, John, 3 5
Shackford, James Atkins, 5, 22, 24, 79, 81, 103, 159, 160, 165, 168, 174, 178, 183, 191, 224, 235, 239
Shelby County, 58
Shoal Creek, 33, 46, 47-51
Siler, Jacob, 15, 149
Sipsey Fork, 116
Smith, Henry, 222, 226, 227
Smith, Seba, 60, 176
St. Francis County, AR, 186
Stiles, John, 196
Stonecipher, Absalom, 7, 28
Stout, Henry, 198, 199
Sullivan County, TN, 5, 10, 153
Sutherland, John, 228-29
Swannanoa Gap, 141
Swannanoa, NC, 54, 65, 135, 136-40

Swannanoa River, 147
Swisher, John Mitchell, 214
Sylacauga, AL, 112-15

Talladega, AL, 109-12
Talladega Springs, AL, 112
Tallapoosa River, 101, 103
Tallasehatchee, AL, 102, 105-8, 160
Tecumseh, 122, 124
Ten Islands, 99, 101, 109
Tennessee General Assembly, 30, 33-34, 35, 36, 49, 50, 52, 53, 54, 67, 70, 76
Tennessee River, 46, 48, 79, 101, 116, 119
Tennessee Vacant Land Bill, 60, 158, 166, 167, 168
Tennessee Volunteer Mounted Riflemen, 39
Tensaw, AL, 124
Texas, Republic of, 136, 212
Thomas, B. Archer M., 217
Thompson's Creek. *See* Honeycomb Creek
Tinkle, Lindsey K., 81, 206
Tipton, John, 4
Tombigbee River, 117, 127
Tookabatcha, 122
Trammel's Trace, 193, 194, 199
Travis, William Barrett, 197, 210, 215, 225, 226, 228, 229, 230, 232, 233, 235
Tremont House, 177
Trenton, TN, 62-65
Trinity River, 198, 212
Tuscaloosa, AL, 116, 119
Tuxedo, NC, 142

Union Hotel, 93

United States Bank. *See* Second United States Bank
United States Hotel, 176, 181, 183

Van Buren, Martin, 168, 178
Vance Birthplace State Historic Site, 137, 138
Vance, David, 144
Vance, Robert Brank, 135, 142-48
Vance-Carson duel, 135, 139, 142-48
Vernon, TN, 56
Viesca, Don Agustin, 204

Walker, Tandy, 122
War of 1812, 123, 196
Warren, Edward, 199
Washington, George, 21, 122
Washington, VA, 12
Washington, AR, 190-91
Washington City. *See* Washington, D.C.
Washington, D.C., 60, 65, 80, 139, 157-69
Washington, GA, 214
Washington County, TN, 5, 10
Washington Tavern, 191
Washington Town Company, 214
Washington-on-the-Brazos, TX, 136, 206, 210, 211, 212-16, 218, 228

Watauga Association, 3, 10
Watauga River, 2, 10
Weakley County, TN, 60, 79, 80
Weatherford, William. *See* Red Eagle
Webster, Daniel, 181, 182
Wells Creek. *See* Wills Creek
Whigs, 59, 80, 162, 174-75, 176, 178, 180-84
Whitaker, Mary Canady, 142
White, Hugh Lawson, 179
White, James, 102
White Rock, TX, 196
White Sticks, 122
Wilderness Road, 11, 153
Wildfire, Colonel Nimrod, 164
Williams, John, 35
Williamson, Robert, 232
Wills Creek, 101
Wilson, Abraham, 18
Winchester, James, 40, 77, 91
Winchester, Marcus B., 62, 88, 91-92
Winchester, Mary, 91
Winchester, TN, 38-40, 43, 96
Winchester, VA, 156
Woodruff, William, 187, 188
Wytheville, VA, 11